TRUTH WARRIORS - 2

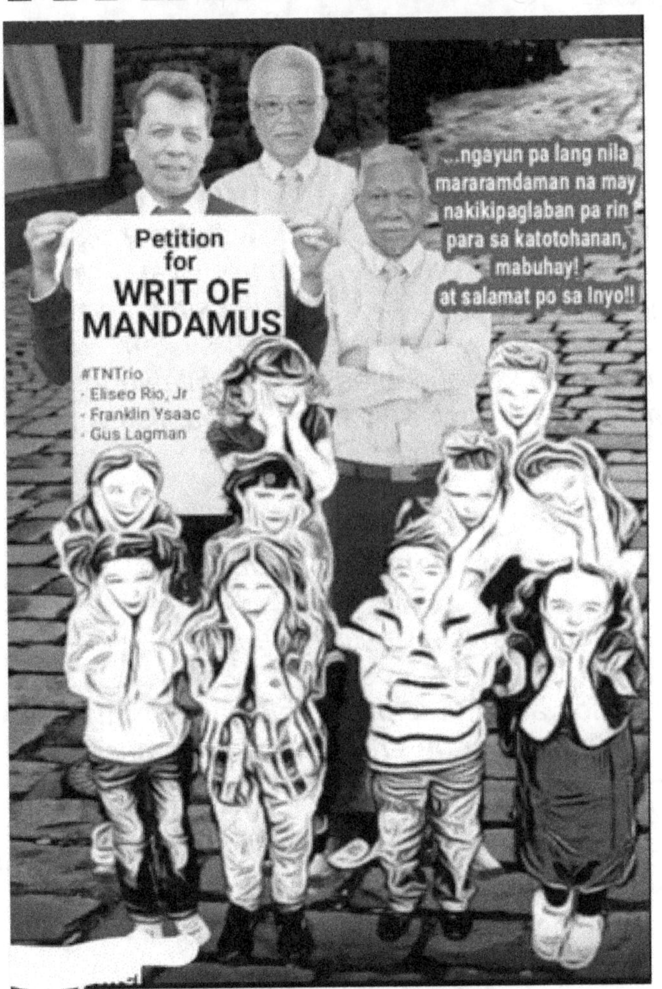

FRANKLIN YSAAC, GEN. ELISEO RIO JR., & GUS LAGMAN

OCTOBER – NOVEMBER, 2022

Published in USA by

TATAY JOBO ELIZES,
*Self-Publisher, under the
permission and authorization of*

Franklin Ysaac
author and copyright owner

*The copyright owner can withdraw this permission at his
discretion without any objection from Tatay Jobo Elizes
at any time. Printing of this book is using the present day
method of Print-On-Demand (POD) system, where prints
will never run out of copies to be available for posterity.
The copyright owner is free to republish with other
publishers anytime.*

**KDP ISBN: 9798362372989
Independently Published**

*Disclaimer: Views are expressed by the author alone.
Tatay Jobo Elizes does not knowingly publish false
information and may not be held liable for the views of
the author and right to free expression.*

*Contact: job_elizes@yahoo.com +
https://www.facebook.com/franklin.ysaac +
http://tinyurl.com/mj76ccq (amazon site) +
www.tatayjoboelizes.webs.com +
https://www.facebook.com/groups/399368500835109*

Content

ooooooo

1
Update – Oct. 15, 2022
3PM, NY Time –
Continuous Prayers by Warriors

Perhaps it's with great pride that a fellow truthwarrior publisher took the cudgel of converting my posts into a book. But that pride took me by surprise as I never imagined the first attempt by our publisher shared me before a set of my earlier posts. I asked him to convert the first attempt into a book so the full story can be told from day 1 when I went public.

I received plaudits and support while others commented that they already read most of my posts since they started following me. Hence, they deferred buying the book. Nonetheless, the publisher offered the book for free and available to those who would forego buying the book.

Since it's free on fb, the book which is a compilation of my posts is a narrative of the search for truth by IT truthwarriors. But keeping the book can be a good story about the truth campaign which can inspire the next generation.

I haven't gone back to day 1 of my posts but as far as I can recall, the story was a full recount of what happened after I started posting my comments about the last election to the latest event.

The book of compilations if you happen to read back gives me and everyone who hasn't read my posts a window to the making of a history written not by me but a history written with the inspiration from the Almighty.

We are nearing already to the finale of the many episodes of this 6 month search.

I compared this 6 month journey to the 6 months of apparitions by the Blessed Virgin to the three children in Fatima. Every 13th of the month starting May 13 through October 13, the three children visited the site in

Fatima where the Blessed Virgin appeared to them and called for penance and prayers by saying the rosary everyday as wars were imminent. WW1, WW2 happened and now WW3 is threatening the world.

Somebody made remarks comparing the #TNTrio to the three musketeers, even to the holy Trinity even if we are not that holy as this comparison is reserved only for God the Father, God the Son and God the Holy Spirit.

We don't mind being called messengers of God as the Holy Spirit has been guiding us in this aftempt to unearth the truth.

We believe that with your continuing prayers and invocation for intervention of our Lord, we will achieve our goal and the truth will soon be ours and the sins of the perpetrators will be uncovered.

When the truth comes out, there will definitely be consequences and we decline to comment on the possible consequences as we leave this matter to our lawyers.

Our task, like Moses, is to lead our compatriots from the bondage of slavery to corrupt officials, plunderers, human rights violators to peaceful transition to freedom of everyone just like what happened during the edsa revolution after the failed snap election that was rigged.

So, this is where we are now and we will challenge the implementers of the rigged election to show proof of transmission reports where 21 M votes were counted during the first hour.

We overheard one comment that if our position is confirmed that there were no transmissions made during the first hour, then the 21M votes should be declared null and void and should be deducted from the 31M votes garnered by the incumbent. In that case, his total score should only be 10M, paving the way for the real winner to the 14M votes of the next candidate.

Such comment may be remote but all options favor the Filipino people whose rights to know the truth may soon happen if we win the case.

So, let's pray that the Holy Spirit enlighten the SC to grant our request. Let's also pray for our brave lawyers who are busy working preparing for the case.

God of Truth, save our country !

Amen.

oooooo

2
Update – Oct. 16, 2022
Comelec meeting

To truthwarriors who want to participate and ask questions in this forum where the guest is the Chair of Comelec, please feel free to ask direct questions other than what we asked already in our communication with them. In the recent responses by comelec to the same questions you sent to them, they gave already their common answer which is " it's under study."

We do not expect any change in his answers if you ask him the same questions as he will be put on the spot .

As far as #TNTrio is concerned, we reserve our right to question him and comelec in court. He should declare under oath whether there were transmissions made and he should show proof of transmissions but not in this forum where he can deny outright.

But we will participate only as observer and we will take note all the questions raised and his answers whether they are truthful or not.

Go ahead and ask him questions but don't identify yourself as truth warrior.

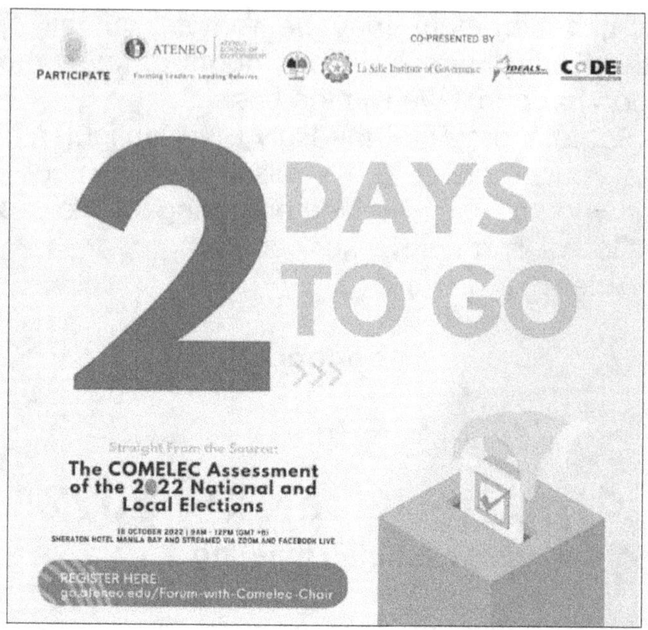

oooooo

3
Update – Oct. 16, 2022,
NY time 10PM
Comelec Forum run-around tactics expected

This is my personal view about tomorrow's forum on election matters where the moderator will be Christian Eaguerra and the resource person is the current comelec chair.

A couple of weeks ago, Christian Eaguerra interviewed spokesman of Comelec and the spokesman made baseless arguments that election was clean and honest. I noted down all his arguments and when we conducted our second presscon we invited Christian to attend our event.

I prepared a list of the arguments of the spokesman and we answered them point by point and I published them here. Throughout the session, Eli described the falsehoods of the arguments but Christian stood silent the whole session. We were informed he was there to observe our presscon.

He left early before the closing of the session.

We were expecting he would present our facts in his "Facts First " program and we were expecting he would give us air time but this never came.

So what gives? Now, Ateneo School of Government invited him to be the moderator with no less than the comelec chair as resource person.

Then we read he likes the explanation of comelec even if he already saw our presentation.

I am not comfortable with this forum at all. I signed up just to listen but it's not my habit to listen to disgraced persons.

So, what will happen tomorrow ? It will be the same set of deflections just like what comelec wrote to us and to many of you.

Again, I will take note and write our rebuttal in this page if we find them to be another round untruths or deflections.

Sagutin lang nila ng derecho kung talaga may transmission at pakita ang proof.

Hindi na Kailangan ang forum na eto!!!!!

oooooo

4
Update, Oct. 17, 2022 –
Comelec Forum today

In today's forum on election matters which will be held at Sheraton, I read the call from some of you to hold picket to protest election irregularites.

This is very encouraging and this small mass action can reverberate to tell the world that the May 9 election was tainted with fraudulent means.

I suggest hold banner of truth and announce to the chair and moderator to just answer our voters petition to show proof of transmission reports. No more lies !

We will join the forum via zoom but we will not actively participate by asking questions. We leave that to truth warriors.

As I said, we will just take notes just like the last interview by CE with Comelec Spox in his program where the views of Comelec were untruths. When we held our own presscon after this interview, we invited CE who obliged to be observer. We answered the points of Comelec Spox and belied his pronouncements point by point . Then , Eli Rio presented the truth behind the irregularities.

Perhaps, CE was not convinced as he remained silent and left before the end of our presscon. We gave him a presscon kit about our presentation . Unfortunately, he didn't announce the details of the kit in his program.

Maybe you can ask him his impression about our presentation re our case in this forum.

If there is no closure to our request for transmission proof, then this forum is just a smokescreen which we will blow when we file our case before SC.

Sabi nga ng mga naniningil Kung may utang ka at ayaw mo magbayad, " Magkita na lang tayo sa korte."

Tayo po maniningil sa Comelec para ilabas ang katotohanan. Yan ang utang nila sa bayan na nilinlang sa nakaraang eleksyon .

OOOOOO

5
Update – Oct. 18, 2022 –
NY time, 9AM –
Comelec Chair – Evasive

Here's my initial report from the forum re election matters with Comelec chair this morning.

The forum lasted more than two hours with Comelec chair sounding off as resource person that the May election was credible and transparent since there weren't many successful election protests. There were other resource persons but what was incredible was the ppcrv lady who just echoed what the chair claimed.

We sent our questions to the moderator and, together with Eli, we sent our questions which were technical matters. Culex of Bunyog raised the matter with regard to transmission reports.

Let me just make my assessment of the 2022 election assessment by Comelec.

The chair was just appointed last August and on the questions such as transmission reports, he said he would refer them to their IT department.

We could not get much from an election lawyer who does not have any experience on IT matters. That's why I asked the host, Ateneo, to hold another session with only IT as participants, namely comelec IT, smartmatic, Namfrel, even ppcrv and other IT experts to once and for all settle the irregularities in the automated election system.

A highlight of the session when the question on telco was raised, he said he would check the contract with telcos and he would demand from telcos copies of CDRs which he was not very familiar with.

He also mentioned he would get the transmission data with regard to the first hour as he claimed they have.

Let's see what happens next.

Bitin but at least those items were revelations and he promised he would be cooperative as he invited the audience to the election summit in January 2023.

Otherwise, no clear answer on our request.

That's what I said and feared. Dapat Meron kasama sa resource person his IT department and smartmatic.

For your info.

oooooo

6

Update – Oct. 18, 2022 –
3 Letters

Today has been a heavy working day for #TNTrio and our lawyers.

We spent more than 2 hours listening, reacting and throwing IT questions which the comelec chair was unable to categorically answer. His recorded answers were he would consult with his IT department re transmission data. And he would call on telco to give us CDRs .

Well, we will write him and call on his commitment to show us transmission logs and CDRs even as we finished these letters to telcos to keep the logs of transmission beyond the mandatory 6 month hold on the logs prior to deletion.

These letters will be delivered tomorrow.

18 October 2022

DITO CME Holdings
Attention: President *Ernest R. Alberto*
21st Floor UDENNA Tower
Rizal Drive corner 4th Avenue
Bonifacio Global City 1634 Taguig

Dear DITO Telecommunity:

This is a patriotic request for preservation of subscriber and cyber traffic data integrity of the national election results transmitted from 7PM to at least 9PM of 09 May 2022, within your network.

The Election Automation Law {Republic Act № 8436 Section 27 as amended by Republic Act № 9369 Section 27 effective since 10 February 2007} requires the COMMISSION ON ELECTIONS (COMELEC) and the COMELEC ADVISORY COUNCIL (CAC) to monitor / evaluate / implement the Election Automation Law and submit a report within six months from the date of election to the JOINT CONGRESSIONAL OVERSIGHT COMMITTEE (JCOC) for Electoral Reforms. NATIONAL TELECOMMUNICATIONS COMMISSION (NTC) Memorandum Circular № 2007-04-06 requires public telecommunication entities to retain telecommunication traffic data log. The Cybercrime Prevention Law (effective after 12 September 2012) (specifically Republic Act № 10175 Section 13) requires preservation of subscriber information and traffic data integrity for at least six months.

Previous COMELEC reports to the JCOC had habitually been close to the last day of the "six months" period and sometimes even beyond the last day. The reports had a clever excuse for not including relevant cyber traffic data because of their deletion after expiration of six months. Patriotic citizens want to stop this bad habit by requesting earlier preservation of said data.

This request does not violate the Data Privacy Act because it is just a request for data preservation (not for releasing sensitive data to the requesting party). We wish to share more details. Please allow a face-to-face meeting or at least indicate the email/s where you wish to receive details of this request.

Sincerely yours,

Eliseo Mijares Rio Jr.
eliseoriojr27@gmail.com

Augusto "Gus" C. Lagman
guslagman2019@gmail.com

Franklin Fayloga Ysaac
ffysaac@gmail.com

Identical copies of this Letter were sent (will be sent) to:	
Globe Telecom President Ernest L Cu Globe Tower 2nd Street corner 7th Avenue Bonifacio Global City 1634 Taguig	Smart Communications President Alfredo S Panlilio Ramon Cojuangco Building Makati Avenue corner Ayala Avenue Legaspi Village 1200 Makati City
Commission on Elections	8/F Palacio del Gobernador Andres Soriano corner General Luna Intramuros 1002 Manila

18 October 2022

Smart Communications
Attention: President *Alfredo S. Panlilio*
Ramon Cojuangco Building
Makati Avenue corner Ayala Avenue
Legaspi Village 1200 Makati City

Dear Smart Communications:

This is a patriotic request for preservation of subscriber and cyber traffic data integrity of the national election results transmitted from 7PM to at least 9PM of 09 May 2022, within your network.

The Election Automation Law {Republic Act № 8436 Section 27 as amended by Republic Act № 9369 Section 27 effective since 10 February 2007} requires the COMMISSION ON ELECTIONS (COMELEC) and the COMELEC ADVISORY COUNCIL (CAC) to monitor / evaluate / implement the Election Automation Law and submit a report within six months from the date of election to the JOINT CONGRESSIONAL OVERSIGHT COMMITTEE (JCOC) for Electoral Reforms. NATIONAL TELECOMMUNICATIONS COMMISSION (NTC) Memorandum Circular № 2007-04-06 requires public telecommunication entities to retain telecommunication traffic data log. The Cybercrime Prevention Law (effective after 12 September 2012) (specifically Republic Act № 10175 Section 13) requires preservation of subscriber information and traffic data integrity for at least six months.

Previous COMELEC reports to the JCOC had habitually been close to the last day of the "six months" period and sometimes even beyond the last day. The reports had a clever excuse for not including relevant cyber traffic data because of their deletion after expiration of six months. Patriotic citizens want to stop this bad habit by requesting earlier preservation of said data.

This request does not violate the Data Privacy Act because it is just a request for data preservation (not for releasing sensitive data to the requesting party). We wish to share more details. Please allow a face-to-face meeting or at least indicate the email/s where you wish to receive details of this request.

Sincerely yours,

Eliseo Mijares Rio Jr.
eliseoriojr27@gmail.com

Augusto "Gus" L. Lagman
guslagman2019@gmail.com

Franklin Fayloga Ysaac
ffysaac@gmail.com

Identical copies of this Letter were sent (will be sent) to:	
DITO CME Holdings President Ernest R Alberto 21st Floor UDENNA Tower Rizal Drive corner 4th Avenue Bonifacio Global City 1634 Taguig	Globe Telecom President Ernest L Cu Globe Tower 2nd Street corner 7th Avenue Bonifacio Global City 1634 Taguig
Commission on Elections	8/F Palacio del Gobernador Andres Soriano corner General Luna Intramuros 1002 Manila

18 October 2022

Globe Telecom
Attention: President *Ernest L. Cu*
Globe Tower
2nd Street corner 7th Avenue
Bonifacio Global City 1634 Taguig

Dear Globe Telecom:

This is a patriotic request for preservation of subscriber and cyber traffic data integrity of the national election results transmitted from 7PM to at least 9PM of 09 May 2022, within your network.

The Election Automation Law {Republic Act № 8436 Section 27 as amended by Republic Act № 9369 Section 27 effective since 10 February 2007} requires the COMMISSION ON ELECTIONS (COMELEC) and the COMELEC ADVISORY COUNCIL (CAC) to monitor / evaluate / implement the Election Automation Law and submit a report within six months from the date of election to the JOINT CONGRESSIONAL OVERSIGHT COMMITTEE (JCOC) for Electoral Reforms. NATIONAL TELECOMMUNICATIONS COMMISSION (NTC) Memorandum Circular № 2007-04-06 requires public telecommunication entities to retain telecommunication traffic data log. The Cybercrime Prevention Law (effective after 12 September 2012) (specifically Republic Act № 10175 Section 13) requires preservation of subscriber information and traffic data integrity for at least six months.

Previous COMELEC reports to the JCOC had habitually been close to the last day of the "six months" period and sometimes even beyond the last day. The reports had a clever excuse for not including relevant cyber traffic data because of their deletion after expiration of six months. Patriotic citizens want to stop this bad habit by requesting earlier preservation of said data.

This request does not violate the Data Privacy Act because it is just a request for data preservation (not for releasing sensitive data to the requesting party). We wish to share more details. Please allow a face-to-face meeting or at least indicate the email/s where you wish to receive details of this request.

Sincerely yours,

Eliseo Mijares Rio Jr.
eliseoriojr27@gmail.com

Franklin Fayloga Ysaac
ffysaac@gmail.com

Augusto "Gus" C. Lagman
guslagman2019@gmail.com

Identical copies of this Letter were sent (will be sent) to:	
DITO CME Holdings President Ernest R Alberto 21st Floor UDENNA Tower Rizal Drive corner 4th Avenue Bonifacio Global City 1634 Taguig	Smart Communications President Alfredo S Panlilio Ramon Cojuangco Building Makati Avenue corner Ayala Avenue Legaspi Village 1200 Makati City
Commission on Elections	8/F Palacio del Gobernador Andres Soriano corner General Luna Intramuros 1002 Manila

oooooo

7
Update – Oct. 19, 2022 –
Preparing Submission to SC

Hereunder is the latest financial report by our Treasurer in Trust.

Thank you to all who contributed to our fund which is reserved for our legal needs.

Together, we #TNTrio and legal team have been working overtime to complete the mandamus petition on or before the end of this month.

We are adding new developments to our case after we participated in the forum last Tuesday wherein the comelec chair revealed a lot.

That's why I, together with our secretary and treasurer, had to rush delivering the letters to the telcos yesterday as these are necessary documents supportive of our case. Signed copies of these letters will be emailed to the comelec chair to ensure he won't forget his commitment to secure the CDRs from the telcos.

There are more developments from the Tuesday forum where first hand revelations by the comelec chair are being consolidated by #TNTrio as misleading statements will be included in our petition.

We know you are looking forward to an early completion of our petition but we assure you that we are doing painstaking efforts to put together an airtight position so our petition will not be dismissed outright when we file the case.

We are providing our lawyers the necessary funds coming from our and your contributions. We begged their indulgence as we committed to raise additional funds even if they are not asking for the usual acceptance fee which is not a small amount. We are really very grateful to our lawyers who do not leave any stone unturned especially in doing research on our case as they agree this case is unprecedented and there has been no jurisprudence on our case.

As we listened to their opinions, we are more enlightened by the day and we shall share with you any development but we cannot present the body of our petition as this will be telegraphing our position to the other camp.

Please bear with us who are learning more from our case which we started building up since day 1 after the May 9 election.

Our ultimate goal is to discredit and to dump automated election system provided by the current provider and to ensure the future elections will be free, honest, credible and transparent as provided by law as we reveal the irregularities caused by the election system which even the incumbent has called cheating machine.

We, #TNTrio and legal team are ironing out details of our case almost daily as we will still need the imprimatur of a top former justice official who is neutral on the case. We received offers from some lawyers but we cannot accept them as they are still connected with some political parties. We cannot compromise our case if we add them as the SC may consider our case a political case.

Mahirap po etong effort namin and we are glad and confident as we believe that the many months we spent building our case will not go to waste.

Sabi ng isang kasama namin na abogado - " Para sa bayan, para sa kinabukasan ng ating mga kababayan na matapos na ang katiwalian sa ating election"

Pagdasal niyo po kami lalo na mga abogado natin na maliwanagan kami at ang Korte Supreme at ang Comelec para ang katotohanan ay lumabas.

Holy Spirit, we invoke your continuing fire of enlightenment on all the people involved in our case.

Amen.

#		
1	**TRUTH WARRIOR DONATIONS REPORT**	
2	FROM OCT.11, TO 20,2022	
3		
4	PREVIOUS BALANCE	
5	10/11/2022	20,084.38
6		
7	TOTAL DONATIONS RECEIPT	
8	FR. 10/12/22	39,711.62
9		
10	EXPENSE	
11		
12	ATTY'S. FEE	
13	1st. partial	20,000
14	2nd partial	20,000
15		
16	Misc./others	
17	10/12/2022	3,000.00
18	10/18/2022	2,586.10
19		
20		
21	TOTAL OUTSTANDING BALANCE	14,212
22		
23		

oooooo

8
Update – Oct. 20, NY time, 6AM
—
UP Foreign Service class reunion, bathch 71/72

My batchmates from UP Foreign Service Corps '71/72 picked me from my residence this morning for a renunion at the San Pablo residence of retired Ambassador and also an alumnus of Ateneo de San Pablo.

I didn't know they were my followers and as usual they want me to update them with our latest action re mandamus case.

After a sumptuous Laguna flavored lunch, we reminisced about the rally days before and during martial law and graduated without any ceremonies.

After the usual banter and bashing of our former professors, they grilled me on the possible outcome of our truth campaign.

I regretted not accepting their friend requests and they just follow my posts.

At the end, they also contributed to the legal fund.

Thank you Ambassador Manalo and my lady Foreign Service Corps batchmates for a wonderful and meaningful reunion after long absence.

Too bad, UP scrapped the course and offered Masters in International Studies instead.

See you next reunion and will update you on latest mandamus case.

ooooooo

9
Update – Oct. 20, 2022 –
NY time, 10AM – Funding

I just got back from my San Pablo trip today and our treasurer messaged me that as of latest, from balance of 14k our gcash balance has reached almost 40k. And we have more in the pipeline from those sending their contributions to bank transfer.

At the rate we are receiving your humble donations, we will reach our target of 100k legal fund. We have already released 40K and from the balance of 40k we will give 30k more to reach 70k.

Somebody remarked we may not be able to hit the target amount from small contributions from our followers.

This is a group effort and this is volunteerism only. We do not force our followers to contribute. To those who contribute modest amount and big amount , Maraming Salamat po.

We have already many supporting documents including our affidavits and hopefully we shall be ready with the full draft this coming Monday. We shall submit this formal petition to an ex Justice/ representative who may represent us formally before the SC.

We shall be tapping some big donors also in the event we will run short of the target amount of 100k.

To those who expressed doubts about the success of our case, we believe the SC will grant our simple request as it's not political question .

Thank you for all your contributions and our lawyers are working overtime this weekend to finalize the petition.

Let's all pray to the Holy Spirit to guide them till the end.

Amen.

oooooo
10
Update – October, 3033 –
Lourdes Hipolito Message

Huli ka, Pinocchio!!!
ASON HIPOLITO

Caught you, Pinocchio!!!
ASON HIPOLITO

.

Hide Translation

.

Rate this translation

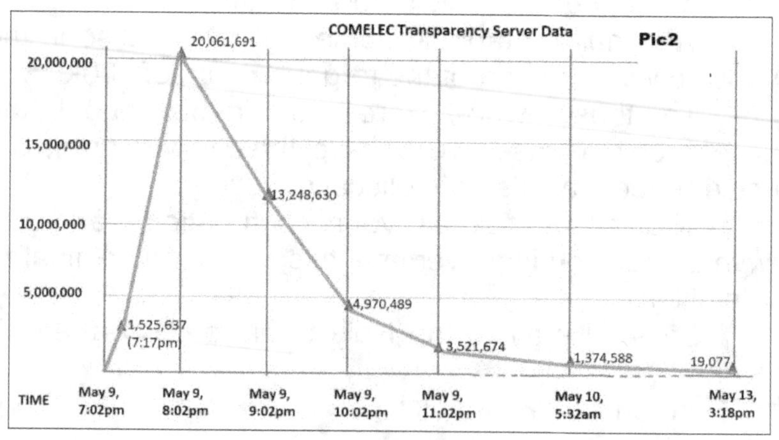

Date/Time	BBM votes	BBM%	Leni votes	Leni%	Paq votes	Paq%	Isko votes	Isko%	Ping votes	Ping%	Total	Hourly +Votes	From/To
May 9/7:02pm	0	0%	0	0%	0	0%	0	0%	0	0%	0	0	
May 9/7:17pm	958,219	63%	409,608	27%	76,668	5%	54,755	4%	26,387	2%	1,525,637		
May 9/8:02pm	12,065,875	60%	5,756,125	29%	957,851	5%	874,188	4%	407,652	2%	20,061,691	20,061,691	7:02pm/8:02pm
May9/8:17pm	15,339,878	60%	7,268,834	29%	1,262,192	5%	1,063,656	4%	505,265	2%	25,459,825		
May9/8:32pm	17,541,799	60%	8,311,501	29%	1,486,592	5%	1,188,776	4%	567,761	2%	29,096,429		
May9/8:47pm	18,975,119	60%	8,979,607	29%	1,639,535	5%	1,268,386	4%	607,251	2%	31,469,898		
May9/9:02pm	20,084,651	60%	9,482,702	28%	1,766,290	5%	1,820,088	4%	636,590	2%	33,310,321	13,248,630	8:02pm/9:02pm
May9/9:17pm	20,978,083	60%	9,921,820	28%	1,879,407	5%	1,378,744	4%	660,178	2%	34,818,232		
May9/9:32pm	21,725,982	60%	10,282,280	28%	1,974,234	5%	1,418,809	4%	679,229	2%	36,080,534		
May9/9:47pm	22,410,199	60%	10,613,144	28%	2,066,021	6%	1,453,828	4%	696,040	2%	37,239,232		
May9/10:02pm	23,017,285	60%	10,915,045	29%	2,152,579	6%	1,485,030	4%	710,871	2%	38,280,810	4,970,489	9:02pm/10:02pm
May9/10:17pm	23,552,108	60%	11,183,118	29%	2,253,664	6%	1,312,344	4%	723,218	2%	39,204,447		
May9/10:32pm	24,070,851	60%	11,447,751	29%	2,316,665	6%	1,538,874	4%	733,999	2%	40,108,140		
May9/10:47pm	24,565,511	60%	11,691,138	29%	2,401,374	6%	1,563,170	4%	744,817	2%	40,966,010		
May9/11:02pm	25,051,855	60%	11,925,131	29%	2,484,310	6%	1,986,319	4%	754,869	2%	41,802,484	3,521,674	10:02pm/11:02pm
May9/11:17pm	25,489,420	60%	12,145,860	29%	2,564,260	6%	1,607,887	4%	763,927	2%	42,571,354		
May10/5:32am	30,223,129	60%	14,400,352	28%	3,451,398	7%	1,839,469	4%	864,197	2%	50,778,545	1,374,588	*
May13/3:18pm	31,104,178	59%	14,822,051	28%	3,629,805	7%	1,900,010	4%	882,236	2%	52,338,277	19,077	**

*From 11:02pm, May9 to 5:32am, May10 (Average per hour for 6.53 hours)
**From 5:32am, May10 to 3:18pm, May13 (Average per hour for 81.76 hours)

Pic1

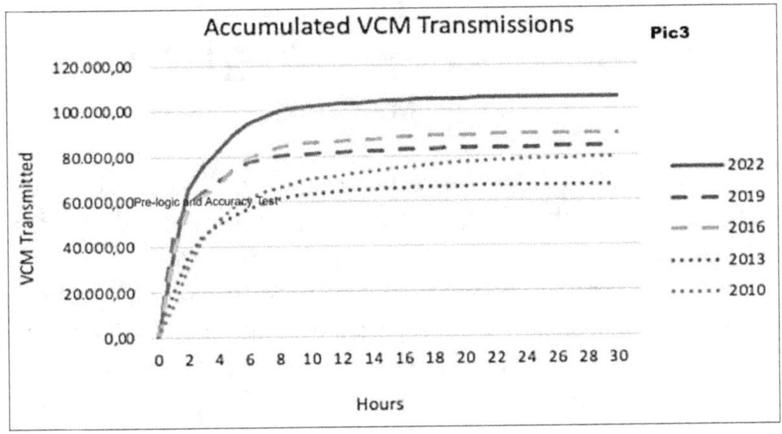

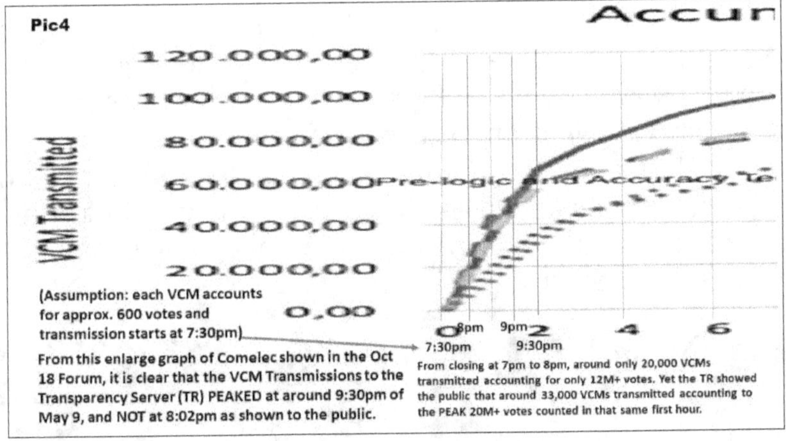

(Assumption: each VCM accounts for approx. 600 votes and transmission starts at 7:30pm)

From this enlarge graph of Comelec shown in the Oct 18 Forum, it is clear that the VCM Transmissions to the Transparency Server (TR) PEAKED at around 9:30pm of May 9, and NOT at 8:02pm as shown to the public.

From closing at 7pm to 8pm, around only 20,000 VCMs transmitted accounting for only 12M+ votes. Yet the TR showed the public that around 33,000 VCMs transmitted accounting to the PEAK 20M+ votes counted in that same first hour.

OOOOOO

11
Update – Oct. 20, 2022 –
NY, 9PM - Books

Lest I forget when I shared my post re the book published by Jobo Elizes to my children in USA, they immediately placed an order with Amazon.

Am sharing photos of my son, Aaron who is working at UN office of Secretary General Gutieres and my granddaughter, Aria, holding copy of my book.

They are asking for my autograph and I said when I fly back there next year after we win our case as there will be a victory sequel naman. Hope and pray so.

Will ask Jobo Elizes if it's okay he can give permission to a local publisher, a UP foreign service corps colleague, who was present in yesterday's reunion so the books can be available locally.

Thank you for patronizing the book and since I am not a subscriber to Amazon, I am yearning also to have a hard copy so I can include my work beside conjugal dictatorship books.

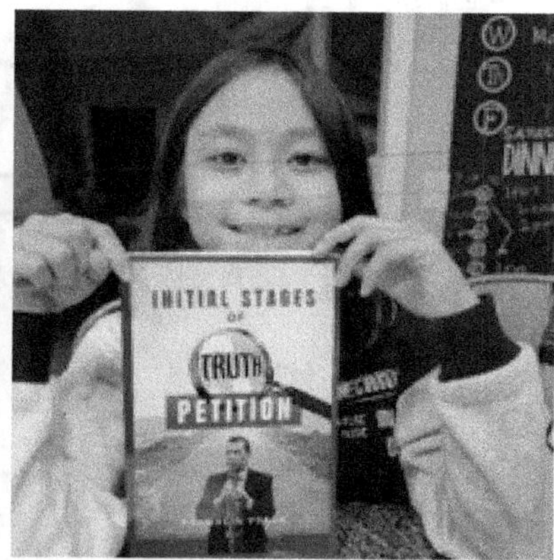

ooooooo

12
Update – Oct. 20, 2022 –
Preparing the Mandamus Petition to SC

Without compromising our position re basis of our mandamus petition, we are reiterating our position which we have been posting in social media.

We are sharing with you our prayer in our mandamus petition.

We enjoin all truth warriors to pray with us that the Supreme Court will grant our petition which is a very simple request for data preservation and disclosure of transmission data during the first hour after closing of election.

The petition, a total of 100 pages, contains hard evidence and exhibits of various jurisprudence and affidavits.

After full review by senior lawyers next week and the petition is approved by them, we shall advise you of date when we will file the mandamus petition before the Supreme Court. This will be any day before the November 9 deadline of telco holdout on the transmission logs.

May the Holy Spirit continue to provide wisdom to our lawyers so the Filipino people will finally see the end of irregularities in the future elections.

Amen.

ISSUES
(PURELY LEGAL ISSUES) / (QUESTIONS OF LAW)

May the Honorable Supreme Court order the respondents to preserve the subscriber / cyber traffic data log integrity / call details records corresponding to national election results transmitted from 7PM to at least 9PM of 09 May 2022?

May the Honorable Supreme Court restrain the respondents from erasing/deleting the subscriber / cyber traffic data log integrity / call details records corresponding to national election results transmitted from 7PM to at least 9PM of 09 May 2022?

May the respondents delay resolution of this case until after the 9th of November 2022 when the respondents are no longer under the duty to preserve said data in accordance with National Telecommunications Commission Memorandum Circular № 2007-04-06 in relation to the Cybercrime Prevention Law (specifically Republic Act № 10175 Section 13)?

May the respondents invoke the Data Privacy Act as excuse notwithstanding the logic that this Petition is just praying for preservation of historically-important data = not release of said historically-important data to the petitioners?

PRAYER

Wherefore the petitioners most respectfully pray for promulgation of timely provisional remedy before the 9th of November 2022 with the following:

1.   Writ of mandamus directing the respondents to retain and preserve the historically-important subscriber / cyber traffic data log integrity / call details records corresponding to national election results transmitted from 7PM to at least 9PM of 09 May 2022.

2.   Writ of mandamus directing the respondents to deliver a secure copy of said historically-important data to the Honorable Supreme Court.

3.   Temporary Restraining Order (TRO) for the respondents to cease and desist from erasing/deleting the said historically-important data.

Petitioners pray for other relief which the Honorable Supreme Court may deem best for the People of the Philippines.

oooooo

13
Update – October 22, 2022 –
Attendance requested

It has come to my attention that there are some truthwarriors who want to be present at the SC when we file our mandamus petition.

We know this is historic and unprecedented according to our lawyers as there has never been a case like this that was filed before the SC and with Comelec, Smartmatic and the three telcos as respondents.

Since it's an ordinary filing and there is no hearing date yet, we will appreciate it very much if you could give us moral support with your presence. But we don't encourage that we wear our party colors because that may be considered as partisan activity and SC may not favor us with the request we want.

We will advise you one or two days before our scheduled filing date and time.

Maraming Salamat po.

oooooo

14
Update – Oct. 22, 2022 –
NY 5PM – "Loose Lips Sink Ships"

" Loose lips sink ships".
Remember these words ?
Sa pagkakataon nag pag sasaliksik namin nung unang lumabas ang resulta ang election na Hindi kapanipaniwala, puro speculative pa kami kasi Wala pa kami matigas at solid na ebidensiya. Nung analyze namin ang proceso ang automated election ng smartmatic, Wala talaga transparency kasi Hindi nakita

ng lahat ang pag bilang ng balota at Di paglabas ng transmission, nag konek mga pirapiraso sa pag buo ng aming findings na talaga kadudada ng eleksyon.

Nag ikot kami sa mga bawat imbitasyon sa amin tatlo dito at sa abroad at nilabas namin observation na Maraming irregularidad.

Marami Hindi naniwala sa amin kasi Wala kami hard evidence .

Totoo Wala pa kami napulot na hard evidence.

Tapos unti unti nadidikit namin ang ebidensiya .

Papano?

Dahil sa mga pagsulat namin sa comelec at sa mga sulat ninyo sa comelec , nililihis mga sagot na under study at kung Saan Saan kami tinuturo

Para hanapin ang Tama ng sagot.

Hanggang sa huli nung martes sa 2022 eleksyon Assessment nag salita na ang chair ang ppcrv at iba pa . Sa pananalita ng chair Marami siya inamin na tungkol sa mga katanungan namin. Sabi niya hihingin niya CDRssa telco Kaya sumulat agad kami sa telco na wag delete ang CDRs . Tapos pinakita graph ng transmission data na eto ngayon analyze ng magaling namin na si General Rio at sa graph po nakita namin Hindi talaga Pwede lumabas ang 21M boto ng incumbents . Tapos sagot niya papa kita niya na Meron transmission logs Sa transparency server.

Ngayon imposible sa graph na galing sa kanila na umabot na 21 M bilang na balita.

Kaya nag papa Salamat po kami Kay chair na mamadali ang kaso natin dahil Galing din sa kanila ang Gagamitin namin ebidensiya against them.

Kaya nga ang kasabihan. " Loose lips sink ships" ay malaking bagay at ginhawa sa kaso natin. At Dagdag natin eto sa ebidensiya sa kaso natin.

Maraming Salamat po chair.

See Translation

" Loose lips sink ships".

Remember these words ?

At the time when we were researching when the election results were first released that were unbelievable, we were still speculative because we don't have hard and solid evidence. When we analyzed the process of the automated election of smartmatic, there was really no transparency because not everyone saw the counting of the ballots and when the transmission came out, the piracy connected to formulate our findings that are really confusing of election.

We went around every invitation of the three of us here and abroad and we made an observation that there are many irregularities.

Many didn't believe in us because we don't have hard evidence.

True, we haven't collected any hard evidence yet.

Then little by little we stick to the evidence .

Daddy?

Because of our comelec writings and your comelec letters, the answers that are under study are diverted and where we are being pointed

To find the right answer.

Until the end of Tuesday in the 2022 election Assessment, the chair, the PPCRV and others have already spoken. In the chair's speech he admitted a lot about our questions. He said he will ask for CDRs from Telco, so we immediately wrote to Telco not to delete the CDRs. Then the graph of the transmission data was shown, now analyzed by our good General Rio and in the graph we saw that 21M votes of incumbents cannot come out. Then his answer dad saw that there are transmission logs in the transparency server.

Now it's impossible for a graph from them to reach 21 M numbers of news.

That's why we are thanking the chair that our case will be faster because we will use evidence against them.

That's why the saying goes. " Loose lips sink ships" is a big deal and a relief to our case. And let's add this to the evidence in our case.

Thank you very much, chair.

oooooo

15
Update – Oct, 22, 22
NY, 6PM – Followup letter to Comelec.

This letter is a follow up to the remarks by Comelec Chair George Gracia in yesterday's forum on 2022 election assessment.

Let's pray he responds positively to this follow up letter. Fyi.

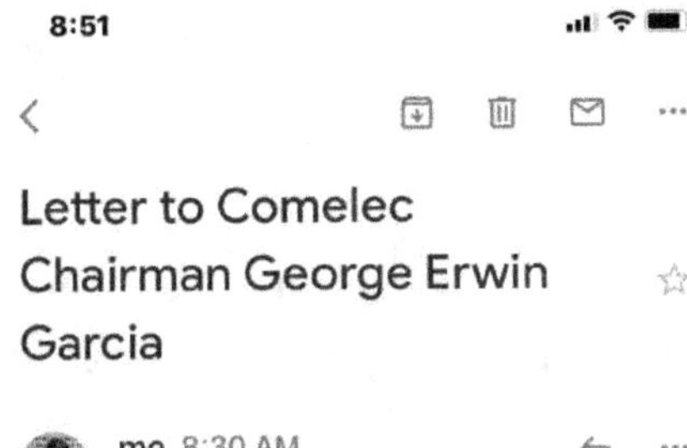

8:51

Letter to Comelec Chairman George Erwin Garcia

me 8:30 AM
to clerkofthecommission, c... ⌄

Commission on Elections
Manila

Attention: Chairman George Erwin
Mojica Garcia

Honorable Chairman,

This refers to your statements during the Ateneo sponsored Election 2022 Assessment last October 18, 2022.

I like to congratulate you for making the effort to reach out and explain the role of Comelec in making the election transparent.

As IT expert and participant in that forum, I raised several issues regarding the conduct of the May 2022 election which you responded with some reservations.

I appreciate your candidness when you mentioned that you will be providing us transmission logs from the transparency server during the first hour, more specifically from 7 to 8 pm, on May 9, 2022 after the closing of election hour. Secondly, you mentioned further that you will secure from telcos call detail reports (CDRs) or transmission logs during the first hour from 7 to 8 pm on May 9, 2022.

In the interest of transparency, I will appreciate it very much if you can provide us soft copies of said
 documents.

I am leaving my email address where you can send said files. It's
ffysaac@gmail.com.

Thank you very much.

Very truly yours,

Franklin Ysaac
President
Franklin Financials Consultancy Phils Inc.
Past President of Financial Executives Institute of the Philippines

oooooo

16
Update – Oct. 22, 2022 –
NY time, 11PM –
Comelec Chairman Garcia Statements

Sharing po etong Tagalog version kung Bakit Kailangan mag paliwanag ang comelec sa kadudadudang resulta.

Yung graph po galing sa comelec at hindi mag tugma ang 21M sa unang oras pagkatapos ng eleksyon kasi sa graph nila mga 12 M lang ang Dapat bilang.

Ano kasabihan ay " a fish is caught by its own mouth " ay nagpapatunay na pag sinungaling ka Mahuhuli ka sa kadaldalan mo.

Basahin po niyo eto at kung maniwala po kayo Yan din po kasama sa dokumento sa petition natin.

Sharing this Tagalog version on Why comelec needs to explain the doubtful results.

The graph is from comelec and the 21M will not match in the first hour after the election because in their graph only 12M should be counted.

The saying "a fish is caught by its own mouth" proves that if you are a liar, you will be caught by your talk….

See more Eliseo Rio Jr. article below,

Date/Time	BBM votes	BBM%	Leni votes	Leni%	Paq votes	Paq%	Isko votes	Isko%	Ping votes	Ping%	Total	Hourly +Votes	From/To
May 9/7:02pm	0	0%	0	0%	0	0%	0	0%	0	0%	0	0	
May 9/7:17pm	958,219	63%	409,608	27%	76,668	5%	54,755	4%	26,387	2%	1,525,637		
May 9/8:02pm	12,065,875	60%	5,756,125	29%	957,851	5%	874,188	4%	407,652	2%	20,061,691	20,061,691	7:02pm/8:02pm
May9/8:17pm	15,339,878	60%	7,288,034	29%	1,262,192	5%	1,063,656	4%	505,265	2%	25,459,825		
May9/8:32pm	17,541,799	60%	8,311,501	29%	1,486,592	5%	1,188,776	4%	567,761	2%	29,096,429		
May9/8:47pm	18,975,119	60%	8,979,607	29%	1,639,535	5%	1,268,386	4%	607,251	2%	31,469,898		
May9/9:02pm	20,084,651	60%	9,482,702	28%	1,766,290	5%	1,330,088	4%	636,540	2%	33,310,321	13,248,630	8:02pm/9:02pm
May9/9:17pm	20,978,083	60%	9,921,820	28%	1,879,407	5%	1,378,744	4%	660,178	2%	34,818,232		
May9/9:32pm	21,725,982	60%	10,282,280	28%	1,974,234	5%	1,418,809	4%	679,229	2%	36,080,534		
May9/9:47pm	22,410,199	60%	10,613,144	28%	2,066,021	6%	1,453,828	4%	696,040	2%	37,239,232		
May9/10:02pm	23,017,285	60%	10,915,045	29%	2,152,579	6%	1,485,030	4%	710,871	2%	38,280,810	4,970,489	9:02pm/10:02pm
May9/10:17pm	23,552,103	60%	11,133,118	29%	2,233,664	6%	1,512,344	4%	723,218	2%	39,204,447		
May9/10:32pm	24,070,851	60%	11,447,751	29%	2,316,665	6%	1,538,874	4%	733,999	2%	40,108,140		
May9/10:47pm	24,565,511	60%	11,691,138	29%	2,401,374	6%	1,563,170	4%	744,817	2%	40,966,010		
May9/11:02pm	25,051,855	60%	11,925,131	29%	2,484,310	6%	1,586,319	4%	754,869	2%	41,802,484	3,521,674	10:02pm/11:02pm
May9/11:17pm	25,489,420	60%	12,145,860	29%	2,564,260	6%	1,607,887	4%	763,927	2%	42,571,354		
May10/5:32am	30,223,129	60%	14,400,352	28%	3,451,393	7%	1,839,469	4%	864,197	2%	50,778,545	1,374,588	*
May13/3:18pm	31,104,175	59%	14,822,051	28%	3,629,805	7%	1,900,010	4%	882,236	2%	52,338,277	19,077	**

*From 11:02pm, May9 to 5:32am, May10 (Average per hour for 6.53 hours)

**From 5:32am, May10 to 3:18pm, May13 (Average per hour for 81.76 hours)

Pic1

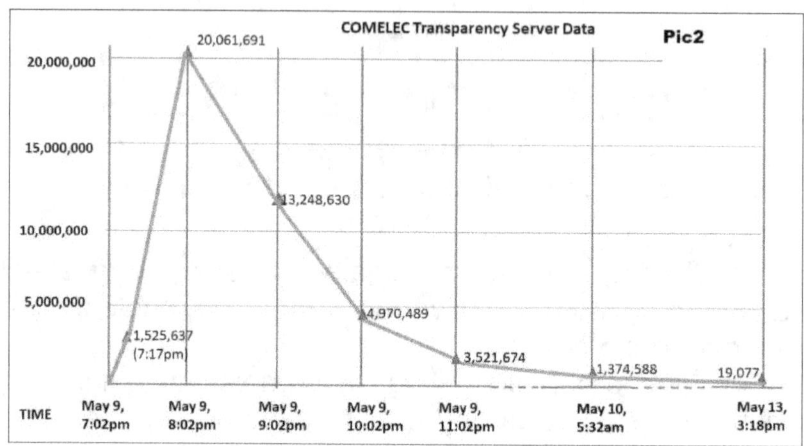
COMELEC Transparency Server Data
Pic2
20,061,691
20,000,000
15,000,000
10,000,000
5,000,000
13,248,630
1,525,637
(7:17pm)
4,970,489
3,521,674
1,374,588
19,077
TIME
May 9, 7:02pm
May 9, 8:02pm
May 9, 9:02pm
May 9, 10:02pm
May 9, 11:02pm
May 10, 5:32am
May 13, 3:18pm

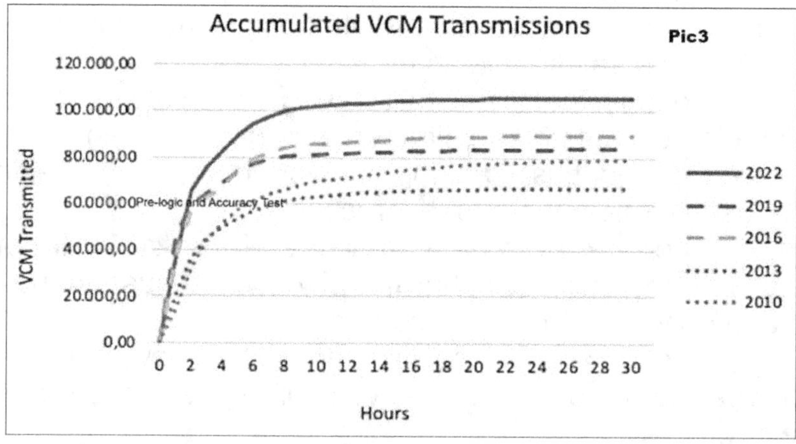
Accumulated VCM Transmissions
Pic3
120.000,00
100.000,00
80.000,00
60.000,00
40.000,00
20.000,00
0,00
Pre-logic and Accuracy Test
VCM Transmitted
0 2 4 6 8 10 12 14 16 18 20 22 24 26 28 30
Hours
2022
2019
2016
2013
2010

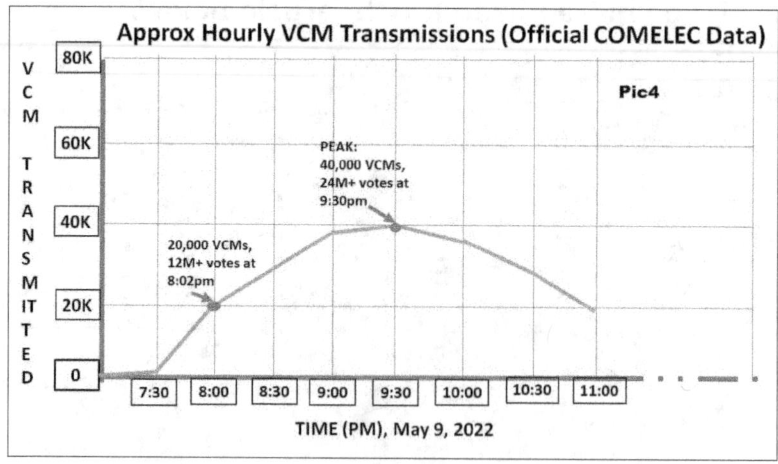
Approx Hourly VCM Transmissions (Official COMELEC Data)
Pic4
V C M   T R A N S M I T T E D
80K
60K
40K
20K
0
PEAK:
40,000 VCMs,
24M+ votes at
9:30pm
20,000 VCMs,
12M+ votes at
8:02pm
7:30 8:00 8:30 9:00 9:30 10:00 10:30 11:00
TIME (PM), May 9, 2022

By Eliseo Rio Jr.

Noong July 15, 2022, sumulat kami sa COMELEC tungkol sa aming pagsusuri na dapat nilang mapatunayan, sa pamamagitan ng pagpakita ng aktuwal na TRANSMISSION LOGS, na ang kanilang Transparency Server ay nakapagbilang ng pinakamalaking boto (PEAK COUNT) na mahigit 20 MILYON sa unang oras pa lamang ng pagbibilang mula 7PM to 8PM; at 13.2 MILYONG boto lang nang ikalawang oras mula 8PM to 9PM ng Mayo 09, 2022. Pagkatapos ng unang oras, ang mga sumunod na bilang cada oras ay makikitang may kataka-takang CONSTANT VOTE RATIO para sa LAHAT ng kandidato sa pagka-Presidente at Bise-Presidente, at hindi nagbago ang mga ratio sa loob ng 4 na araw ng pagbibilang.

Ang gayong resulta (Pic 1 and Pic 2), kung pagbabasehan ang Mathematics, Lohika at Statistics, ay malamang na HINDI TOTOO, kung hindi man IMPOSIBLE.

Ang Pangkalahatang Direktiba ng COMELEC sa mga guro na tumatao sa bawat presinto bilang Board of Election Inspectors (BEI) ay unahin munang mag-PRINT ng (😎 WALONG KOPYA ng Election Returns (ER) BAGO pa man gumawa ng kahit anong transmission sa Transparency Server. Ngunit sa Time and Motion Studies, makikita na ang hinihinging pag-print ng 8 kopya ng ERs ay gugugol ng 30 minuto o baka mahigit pa sa 1 oras. Kaya sa nakaraang botohan nung Mayo na nagsara ng 7:00PM, ang pinaka-maagang transmission ay maaaring nasa bandang 7:30PM na. Hanggang ngayon, ang aming liham ay hindi pa rin nasasagot ng maayos.

Noong October 18, 2022, may isinagawang FORUM ang Ateneo School of Government: COMELEC ASSESSMENT of the May 2022 National and Local Elections, kung saan si COMELEC Chairman George

Garcia ang pangunahing tagapag-salita. Sa forum na iyon, may ipinakitang graph na isinalarawan ang mga Vote-Counting Machine (VCM) Transmissions ng ilang mga nagdaang eleksiyon [Accumulated VCM Transmissions] (Pic 3).

Sa malapitang pagsisiyasat, makikita na yung resulta ng May 2022 Elections na ipinakita sa publiko ng Transparency Server ay MAY MATINDING IREGULARIDAD at hindi tumutugma sa VCM Transmission data sa Pic3.

Ang cada-oras na VCM Transmission na hinango sa COMELEC Transmission graph (Pic 4) ay nakapagpapakita ng mas regular na transmission kaysa sa pinakikita ng Transparency Server (Pic2). WALANG PEAK COUNT na +20 MILYONG BOTO ang naipakita sa 8:02PM. Ang rurok ng bilangan ay nangyari bandang 9:30PM ng Mayo 09,2022.

KAYA SAAN NAGMULA ANG MGA KUWESTIYONABLENG DATOS NA PINAKITA SA PUBLIKO NG TRANSPARENCY SERVER?

Nang aming tinanong tungkol sa Peak 20M+ na boto at ang kaduda-dudang constant vote ratio ng lahat ng kandidato para sa pagka-Presidente at Bise-Presidente, walang patumanggang sinabi ni Chairman Garcia na iyong 20M+ na boto ay nagmula sa PPCRV at HINDI SA COMELEC! 😊

Ang isa pang katanungan na hindi nasagot ay kung masisiguro ba ng COMELEC sa mga botante na yung MGA KAHON NG BALOTA ay napili ng pagkakataon lang (randomly) at hindi nagalaw ninuman habang binibiyahe papuntang Diamond Hotel para sa Random Manual Audit, dahil ang mga TAGA-BANTAY para sa aktibidad na iyon—ang NAMFREL AT LENTE, ay kahit kailan ay hindi nasaksihan ang WASTONG PAGSASARA NG MGA BALLOT BOXES at sila lamang dapat ang makakapag-bukas ng MGA SELYO NG BALLOT BOXES sa pagdating ng mga ito sa Diamond Hotel.

Sa Forum, sinabi ng tagapag-salita ng PPCRV na ang Official Count ng COMELEC ay higit 99% na eksakto (accurate), ngunit ang pagsusuri ng PPCRV ay mula sa irregular at kuwestiyonableng datos ng Transparency Server, na ayon kay Chairman Garcia ay kontrolado ng PPCRV!

At ang mga botante ay hindi nabigyan ng kasiguruhan na ang mga balota ay hindi ginalaw ninuman habang binibiyahe mula sa iba't ibang parte ng bansa papuntang Diamond Hotel.

Ang natapos na FORUM ay mas lalong nagdulot na karagdagang tanong at pagdududa sa mga Pilipinong umasa ng MALINAW, EKSAKTO, MAKATOTOHANAN AT KAPANI-PANIWALANG May 09 National and Local Elections.

On July 15, 2022, we wrote to COMELEC about our analysis that they must prove, by showing actual TRANSMISSION LOGS, that their Transparency Server counted the largest votes (PEAK COUNT) over 20 MILLION in just the first hour of counting from 7PM to 8PM; and only 13.2 MILLION votes for the second hour from 8PM to 9PM on May 09, 2022. After the first hour, the following numbers per hour will be seen with a mysterious CONSTANT VOTE RATIO for ALL Presidential and Vice Presidential candidates, and the ratios remained unchanged for 4 days of counting.

Such a result (Pic 1 and Pic 2), if based on Mathematics, Logic and Statistics, is probably NOT TRUE, if not IMPOSSIBLE.

The COMELEC General Directive to teachers acting in each precinct as Board of Election Inspectors (BEI) is to PRINT (😎 EIGHT COPIES of Election Returns (ER) BEFORE making any transmission to Trans. Parenthood Server. But in Time and Motion Studies, it would appear that the required printing of 8 copies of ERs would take 30 minutes or maybe more than 1 hour. So with the last poll in May that closed at 7:00PM, the earliest transmission may have been around 7:30PM. Until now, our letter has not been properly answered.

On October 18, 2022, the Ateneo School of Government held a FORUM: COMELEC ASSESSMENT of the May 2022 National and Local Elections, where COMELEC Chairman George Garcia was the keynote speaker. In that forum, a graph is displayed that illustrates the Vote-Counting Machine (VCM) Transmissions of several past elections [Accumulated VCM Transmissions] (Pic 3).

In a closer investigation, it will be seen that the result of May 2022 Elections that were shown to the public by Transparency Server HAS EXTREME IRREGULARITY and does not correspond to the VCM Transmission data in Pic3.

The hourly VCM Transmission measured in the COMELEC Transmission graph (Pic 4) shows a more regular transmission than the Transparency Server (Pic2). NO PEAK COUNT of +20 MILLION VOTES shown at 8:02PM. The counting peak occurred at 9:30PM on May 09,2022.

SO WHERE DID THE QUESTIONABLE DATA SHOWN TO THE PUBLIC BY THE TRANSPARENCY SERVER COME FROM?

When we asked about Peak 20M+ votes and the dubious constant vote ratio of all the candidates for President and Vice President, Chairman Garcia said no objection that your 20M+ votes came from PPCRV and HI LET'S GO! 😊

Another question left unanswered is whether the COMELEC will assure voters that the BALLOT BOXES were randomly selected (randomly) and not moved while traveling to the Diamond Hotel for the Random Manual Aud it, because the GUARDS for activity that that— NAMFREL AND LENTE, have never witnessed the PROPER CLOSING OF BALLOT BOXES and only they should be able to open the BALLOT BOXes STAMPS upon arrival at Diamond Hotel.

At the Forum, PPCRV spokesperson said COMELEC's Official Count is more than 99% accurate, but PPCRV's analysis is from irregular and questionable data of Transparency Server, which Chairman Garcia said was contravenous wave of PPCRV!

And voters were not assured that the ballots were not moved by anyone while travelling from different parts of the country to Diamond Hotel.

The finished FORUM brought even more questions and doubts to Filipinos who hoped for CLEAR, ACCURATE, TRUTHFUL AND CREDIBLE May 09 National and Local Elections.

oooooo

17
Update – Oct. 23, 2022 –
Lawyers Schedule

Tomorrow, #TNTrio will be meeting with new batch of lawyers who will assist us in the filing of the mandamus case. They will specifically look at all the angles of the case. These lawyers come from different law firms.

When I was still connected with the banks, I used to deal with our external lawyers from big law firms. Aside from retainer fees, we pay them per hour for any opinion we ask from them.

But that is coming from banks where interests of the bank like foreclosure etc cost money and recovery.

In our present case, this is not a case where we #TNTrio will materially benefit as this is case of citizens exercising their freedom of information and this is enshrined in our constitution. Looking for this new batch of lawyers who are experts in constitutional law and election laws are not that easy to find.

We impressed upon them to be lenient with us as to the amount we will share with them because para sa bayan po eto. Luckily, they offered less than what they normally charge.

It's a blessing that we were able to get these lawyers who are patriots also like us.

Kami po #TNTrio from day 1, we give our best without expecting anything except the truth from our campaign. Even my own children are asking me if I draw anything or some kind of remuneration as I have been spending more time on the case. Same with former Namfrel chair Gus Lagman and General Eli Rio. In fact kami pa naglalabas pang Gastos sa mga early meetings. But for the prescons we solicited from our friends as the cost is not small.

At the current stage now, the petition is already finished but we need to allow new lawyers to give their opinions or how to make the case a winnable case. We are also expecting some suggestions from retired members of the judiciary.

We are thankful to these lawyers who have the same commitment as we have but we obliged to give them compensation for their well spent time to make the case a success.

We will be dispensing more for their efforts but unfortunately we had problems with gcash of our treasurer even as we were able to raise more than 100k for the current lawyers in just a few weeks.

Now, our treasuer volunteered my gcash account which I hardly use.

After checking the latest balance, we received more than 15k just for today. We are on our way to the next 100k so we can pay the services of our lawyers including the new batch.

Let's all invoke the Holy Spirit as He is also double timing working with our lawyers.

Personally, I have never seen how these lawyers go out of their way to make sure the case is airtight and worth winning.

Maraming Salamat po sa tulong niyo and malapit na po ang filing natin Baka early next week or first week of November. We will advise you two days before filing date po.

oooooo

18
Update – Oct. 14, 2022 –
NY Time, 9AM – Teleradyo talk between Comelec Chairman and Usec Eli Rio

Just finished watching the hearing via teleradyo between Usec Eli Rio and comelec Spox.

This is my immediate comment.

1. Usec Eli is only asking for transmission reports generated by transparency server and or comelec central server during the first hour after poll closing. It took comelec one month before it responded to our letter, advising us to proceed to CAC and JCOCAE. We did as they requested us. We wrote the CAC and JCOCAE and until now we haven't received any response. Then our followers wrote the same letter we sent last July 15 and comelec patented response was " it's under study ".

2. Comelec Spox didn't answer categorically the question. He even challenged that if any Tom, Dick and Harry requested for the voluminous documents, comelec can't provide them such documents.

My comments are as follows:

1. Usec Eli is asking an IT process of election and transmission reports are available and yet the Spox wouldn't commit to provide him.

2. Comelec Spox is evasive throughout his explanation. He couldn't even figure out the two servers which show two conflicting data with transparency server showing more than 20M and comelec graph which was shown last Tuesday with 12M. Obviously, this is a case where the Spox who is a lawyer doesn't understand how the system works. This is the same response from Comelec chair when he couldn't answer directly question about rhe transmission data and he said he will refer the matter to their IT department.

This is the general problem of comelec people . Ang humaharap sa atin ay abogado na Wala naman Alam sa IT. Bilib na bilib sa smartmatic na 99.9 pct accurate kasi yun ang Sabi ng smartmatic .

Now, to test the water, Usec Eli described how the process of election works from sd cards, to printing of ballots to vcm to telco to transparency . Yan lang po.

Being an IT person also like Usec Eli and former Namfrel chair Gus Lagman, our mandamus petition is the only way comelec, telcos and smartmatic can answer our petition in court. And these officials can raise their right hand to attest to their statements.

With this line of presentation by Spox, Sabi nga ni Usec Eli " common sense dictates impossible mangyari ang 20M plus sa first hour."

In court, we will ask the Comelec to present their IT who handled the transparency server and all pertinent matters and we will grill them if they know whether they followed the general instructions.

Then we tell the court whether their explanation is transparent, honest and credible .

Jusko, sarap humarap sa taong Hindi Alam ang sinasabi niya tungkol sa IT.

Kaya nga remember Yung troll na nag challenge sa akin at Sabi niya magaling siyang IT. Okay Sabi ko kung magaling siya hire ko siya at bayaran ko malaki Pero test ko muna siya .

Ganyan po ako mag hire sa mga programmers. Bibigyan ko program at sabihin ko "debug" mo.

Ayun, sagot nga ng troll " Sir, Ano Yung debug".

Block ko na siya baka Yung bug kumalat pa sa computer ko.

Etong comelec Spox, Ganun din . Pa debug ko rin smartmatic system. Mahuhuli natin sila sa sd card / transparency server manipulation.

May Maganda sinabi siya na mag meeting en banc mga commissioners at mag request sa telco save ang transmission log even beyond November 9.

Meanwhile, Mas tumibay pa position natin after etong interview sa Spox .

"Magkita na lang tayo sa korte Suprema " Sabi ng mga abogado natin. At kami mag present ng case ng irregularities.

Mabuhay po tayo at Dasal lahat na Sana madapa pa sila sa mga sagot nila .

Ronnie Adriano Amoroso

SUSPECTS: PPCRV (TRANSPARENCY SERVER), COMELEC (CENTRAL SERVER), SMARTMAGIC, SD CARDS, TRANSMISSION RECEIPTS/REPORTS, TRANSMISSION LOGS, TELCOS CALL DETAIL REPORTS, NAMFREL & LENTE, DENNIS UY F2 LOGISTICS, MASTERMINDS, ET. AL.

oooooo

19

Update – Oct. 24, 2022 –
Expenditures – Help Please

In today's meeting with our lawyers, after we set the date on Thursday, November 3, St Jude Thaddeus day, we covered incidental expenses like filing fee which is estimated at P15k and printing of documents which we estimated to be around P10K as each Justice is entitled to one copy and each comelec commissioner is entitled also to a copy. The respondents are likewise given a copy each. We will also give all reporters a copy each. Each copy contains minimum 100 pages.

After filing, we plan to hold a presscon with mainstream media finally covering our case. We will reserve fund for this.

As to the lawyers fees, we are still working on them as we will be tapping other sources in addition to what we can raise from truth warriors.

As of today, our total fund stands at P39,112.00 which includes gcash balance and bdo deposit.

When our treasurer gets gcash active this coming November, I will transfer management of said fund to her.

For your info.

oooooo

20
Update – Oct. 24, 2022 –
Legal issues

To all,

This is to share with you revised prayer of our petition after this was reviewed by a former Justice.

Our lawyers will continue to review our petition until final filing.

During the meeting, like what I usually do when I am a complainant or respondent to a case, I play the devil's advocate.

This role enhances your case as you can discern options of what your opponent or in this case, what the SC will do to answer your prayer.

For example, questions like " Did you exhaust all administrative remedies before filing the case ?" "What is your personal interest or objective on the case ?" Are you personally being injured if your cause is not granted ?" "Why the urgent motion of your case?" Is any political party behind your case ?"Are you being funded by any political person, a candidate or a losing candidate?"

There are many more questions directed towards the petitioners motive in filing the case.

Our lawyers will be prepared for all these questions during hearing.

May the Holy Spirit provide all the answers to these questions so our cause can be heard and our prayer will be granted !

Amen.

oooooo

21
Update – Oct. 25, 2022 –
The Heat Is On

The heat is on!

Comelec now desperately grasping at straws just to deny us those transmission data.

In the interview with Eli Rio by Tony Velasquez and Karmina Constantino, Eli was just trying to prove whether there were transmissions made during the first hour. Then when it was Comelec's turn, he misdirected us to CAC and JCOCAE. Very convenient excuse.

Nonetheless he admitted to save ang transmission logs sa Comelec. He assured the comelec board will write the telcos to save the CDRs also

Let's see.

For now, the mainstream media has started to take notice of our petition.

We will definitely invite them on November 3 after we have filed the case and hold a presscon.

At least, na papansin na tayo.

NEWS   A3

Ex-DICT chief wants vote log on May 9 polls saved

By Tyrone Jasper C. Piad
@TyronePiad

The former chief of the Department of Information and Communications Technology (DICT) wants the Supreme Court to have the transmission logs on the May 9 elections kept for review, amid a looming deadline on the deletion of the files in accordance with law.

In an interview on Monday, former Information and Communications Technology Secretary Eliseo Rio Jr. said he would file a mandamus petition in the high court this week, so that data on the transmission logs can be kept and verified to check alleged discrepancies in the recording of the May 9 votes.

"The mandamus petition with the SC is just to preserve the transmission logs related to the transmissions of telcos from the VCMs (vote-counting machines) to the transparency server and the Comelec (Commission on Elections) central server," Rio told the Inquirer.

He cited Section 13 of the cybercrime law (Republic Act No. 10175) regarding the "Preservation of Computer Data," which stipulates that data "provided by a service provider shall be preserved for a minimum period of six months from the date of... receipt."

Law enforcement authorities may order "a one-time extension... provided that once [said] data... is used as evidence in a case, the mere furnishing... of the transmittal document to the Office of the Prosecutor shall be deemed a notification to preserve the computer data until the termination of the case."

Otherwise, the data may be deleted six months from their entry—which in the case of the May 9 election data would be on Nov. 9, or 16 days from today.

"We need these transmission logs to clear our observations that there is discrepancy between the transmissions to the transparency server and the central server," Rio said. "If they get deleted by Nov. 9, then all evidence... will be gone."

Peak transmission

Rio explained that the transparency server handled by the Parish Pastoral Council for Responsible Voting (PPCRV), which showed partial and unofficial results, registered more than 20 million votes by 8:02 p.m. on May 9. Comelec data around that time, however, showed that only 12 million votes were transmitted.

He also noted that the PPCRV server saw peak transmission at that particular time, whereas Comelec data showed peak transmission around 9:30 p.m., or over an hour later.

"This is impossible because all VCMs transmit their data... at the same time," he said.

Rio said he had been asking for the transmission logs since July, but Comelec Chair George Garcia presented the data only on Oct. 18, during a forum by the Ateneo School of Government.

He also questioned how the transparency server was able to receive more than 20 million votes in just an hour after voting closed.

In a post on Facebook, he said that "in the whole history of Philippine elections, and maybe in the whole world, this was the first time counting of votes peaked at the very first hour, despite the fact that in that first hour, the Comelec General Instruction required the printing of (eight) copies of the precinct Election Result (ER) before any transmissions can be made."

Rio said printing the ERs took at least 30 minutes.

"The transmission logs will determine if there are irregularities in the transmissions, which in turn will determine if the May 9 election was rigged," he said.

"If Comelec has nothing to hide, why don't they simply show these transmission logs to the public?" he added. INQ

oooooo

22
Update – Oct. 25. 2022 –
Further preparation

Am sharing a comment from one of our truth warriors and let me mention our response to this comment :

From the very start, we approached several lawyers to assist us in our case. The first response was if there is hard evidence, then they will take up the case. Since we didn't have yet hard evidence we were not able to get support . Then some lawyers begged off because they are conflicted, meaning they are handling cases also against the government . Third, if they take up our case, they fear backlash from the present dispensation as they will be branded as opposition.

Hence, we cannot get support from lawyers of political parties nor can we get lawyers from top caliber firms.

But, when we were getting close to the truth, few lawyers who practice without any connection to any law firm and are committed to the truth came to our support .

For the last couple of weeks, since we cannot afford to pay for their legal services, we launched funding campaign. But they only asked for hours they will spend as they will have to hire legal research people to make sure we are on top of the case. We agreed to compensate them for their time because we are taking their man hours from their other cases. That's fair naman. The initial 100k is not enough for lawyers given the present rate of lawyers fees.

Sa totoo lang po, ako po ay na sa software application business. I also charge per hour plus total development cost as i pay my programmers and they are not cheap. I had experts and they left me because of the bigger offers from big tech companies and offers from abroad. But they are thankful to me coz I taught them the concept and logic of my designs. I do all the logic and designs of all my programs. Because of my banking experience, I was able to connect easily with my bank customers. Thus far, i still have existing contracts and this is keeping me busy and alive until this election blunder caught my attention.

As I said, this is battle of the brains of good IT versus bad IT.

Nakialam naman mga comelec lawyers na walang Alam sa IT . Ayan sumabog tuloy at nadulas si chair at si Spox sa forum ng Ateneo at interview ni Tony Velasques at Karmiba Constantino. Gagamitin namin mga kasagutan nila sa ating kaso.

Isang halimbawa mga Kapalpakan pag nag hire ka ng experts sa ibang profession at nilagay mo sa Wala siyang alam. Di ba? A retired police officer appoint Usec sa DoH. Pwede siya as chief ng security . Di ba?

Yung abogado nagpapnggap na may Alam sa IT, sabihin ko mag debug siya ng SD at transparency server !!'

Sa korte Suprema na lang sila mag paliwanag .

Going back to our case.

Our lawyers claim this is unprecedented and maybe earth shaking if our petition is granted. This will the first in Philippine election history . And it will be the first when people win a case against election handlers.

One of the findings of our lawyers is the election laws are all skewed to the government or comelec and non protective of citizens rights. Election laws must be revised to give protection to voters. In our case, there is no transparency at all as we were never able to witness the printing of ballots, the configuration of sd cards, delivery of ballot boxes and the manual counting of ballots .

In other words, the election system is totally flawed with lots of holes and no room for transparency.

It's time we restore the old manual system and adopt the hybrid system.

Meanwhile, we have a battle to fight and we will pursue this relentlessly until we secure approval of our petition.

Ang umaga po ay gumaganda kahit maulan. Buhos po yan ng blessing galing sa taas.

May kasabihan po " Blessing in disguise daw po lahat ng nangyayari ngayon.

Dagdag ko po" Blessing in the skies po".

Amen .

oooooo

23
Update – Oct. 25, 2022 –
9PM NY – Voluminous reports

As usual, this Spox wants to beat around the bush with regard to disclosure of transmission reports.

Voluminous daw ? We know how this transmission report looks like and we have copies which came from ppcrv . Kailangan pa drawing yan?

Now passing the buck to JCOCAE as what they instructed us to do, Bakit sagot nila sa mga truthwarriors when they requested the same transmission reports, this is "under study " . If they were consistent, Dapat send din nila request to JCOCAE .

Comelec officels, make up your mind? Ano sagot niyo pag file namin sa SC? Go to JCOCAE or under study ?

Let's see what happens after we file our case sa SC. Dapat sagutin lang nila . At Bakit hindi ba Pwede pakita sa mga voters kung May transmission nga o Wala . Sila na rin nag publish ng graph na inconsistent sa sinasabi nila.

(copy of letter below)

May 9 polls transmission logs submitted to congressional body

By Ferdinand Patinio October 25, 2022, 5:23 pm

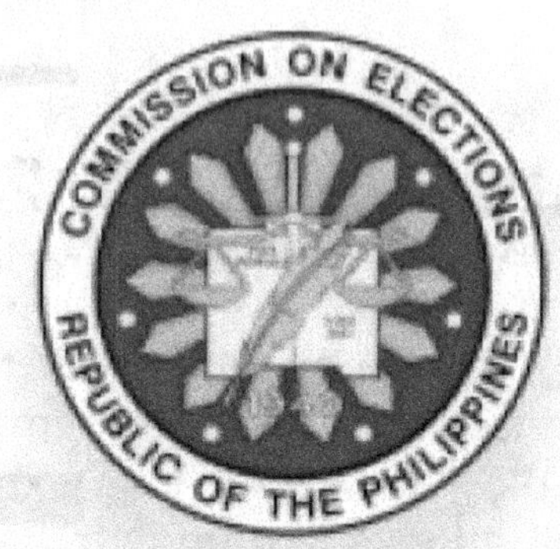

MANILA – The Commission on Elections (Comelec) on Tuesday said transmission logs in connection with the May 9 national and local polls are available before the Joint Congressional Oversight Committee on the Automated Election System (JCOC-AES).

Comelec spokesperson John Rex Laudiangco said those who are asking for a copy of such data can secure it with the said committee.

"This is a voluminous document so we cannot just give it to anyone asking for it. It is better if they get it from the JCOC as this has been submitted under oath and are, therefore, considered as official," he said in a radio interview.

The poll body official noted that the documents were submitted to the JCOC which is required under the law.

On the other hand, he said a request is needed before the Comelec en banc or before the courts with regard to the preservation of the transmission logs beyond six months.

"A request can be made for the Commission en banc to order the further preservation of the data. Interested parties may also go to the Court to seek issuance of precautionary protection order regarding this," Laudiangco added.

Under the Cybercrime Prevention Act of 2012, computer data shall be preserved for a minimum period of six months from the date of the transaction, and authorities may order a one-time extension for another six months before they are allowed to be destroyed.

Laudiangco made the remark after former Department of Information and Communications Technology (DICT) Secretary Eliseo Rio Jr. urged the poll body to provide them with transmission logs in order to verify their observations of discrepancy.

Rio is also planning to file a petition before the Supreme Court to seek the preservation of the transmission logs beyond Nov. 9. *(PNA)*

oooooo

24
Update – Oct. 26, 2022 –
St. Thaddeus

Countdown to Thursday, November 3, just begun today. 7 days to go.

Tomorrow is the feastday of our favorite saint, St Jude Thaddeus, the patron Saint of desperate cases. He was the one who asked during the last Supper: Master, what happened that you will reveal yourself to us and not to the world ? Jesus answered him: Whoever loves me will keep my Word, and my father will love him, and we will come to him and make our dwelling with him (John 14:22-23). He also wrote a letter to the universal Church, known in the Bible as the letter of Jude. He died as a martyr in Persia.

Why do we pray to St Jude?

We pray the novena you St Jude to lead us in prayer for hope and strength during difficult times in our lives and in the lives of others. St Jude sought to love the Lord through challenging times, so we strive to imitate this same unwavering faith.

We enjoin all followers of St Jude especially some of us who feared the worst to come that some bad things may happen after we announced to the world that we are now coming to register a simple petition, that there are bad elements who are out to stop us from filing our case before SC.

Whereas, we were once the case of desperation because of the shock and awe of the May 9 fiasco, little by little we were able to piece together our case so we can have a formal complaint against non full disclosure of the secretive automated election which for several elections became the cheating machine according to the incumbent.

Whereas, many of us have given up the fight already as many didn't know what happened to the election despite the millions who gather during the campaign that grew from small crowd to the biggest crowds throughout the country.

Whereas, while we were not looking, some dirty players picked the wrong time during the pandemic to keep the people from following the process of printing the ballots, delivery of ballot boxes, the non witnessed configuration of sd cards, and the eventual non manual counting of ballots, to the irregular random manual audit process, to the preloaded transmission of votes during the first hour which has become the bone of contention we will file before the SC. This whole process we the #TNTrio without let up conducted our examination until we ended up in the highly irregular and suspicious transmission of more than 20M ballots cast for the incumbent.

Whereas, the mainstream media refused to cover our presscon because of backlash from the incumbent,

To our doubting followers, we are proclaiming that we are on the side of truth.

How else will the whole disenfranchised and disappointed voters know the truth unless we file our case before the SC.

We expect the mainstream media to cover our filing next Thursday and after our spot interview with them we will give them copies of our petition. Since this is now a public case, many political parties will view this as an opportunity to also make their call and may file intervention cases before the SC.

We expect a groundswell of support again just like during the 1986 mass gathering.

Should the SC deny our simple petition, we leave it to the people to decide what to do after.

Praying to St Jude will help us pass this difficult and challenging time so we can all wake up when the SC grants our simple petition.

What follows after the SC grants our petition, the battle for truth will just begin.

There will be hearings but we expect SC to take our motion as urgent as the November 9 deadline before telcos delete the transmission logs is near to our November 3 filing.

St Jude, through your intercession, please make our case a case of hope and not a case of desperation.

Amen.

St. Jude is the Patron Saint of Hope and impossible causes and one of Jesus' original twelve Apostles.

He preached the Gospel with great passion, often in the most difficult circumstances. Through the power of the Holy Spirit, he made profound differences in people's lives as he offered them the Word of God. The Gospel tells us that St. Jude was a brother of St. James the Less, also one of the Apostles. They are described in the Gospel of Matthew as the "brethren" of Jesus, probably cousins. St. Jude is often confused with Judas Iscariot who betrayed Jesus.

oooooo

25
Update – Oct. 26, 2022
Gen. Eliseo Riro Jr.

Meet " The Man of the Hour ". A true gentleman. A doting father and grandfather. An IT par excellence with electrical/ electronics/ communication engineering background. A quintessential government official with uncompromising principles. A military General,nurtured by a family of military officers, a UP Vanguard Corps Commander who became ISAFP head. A Man with a Destiny and Legacy to the Nation as advocate for clean, honest and transparent election.

This gentleman is truly " A man for all seasons". A man who is ready to cope with any contingency and whose behavior is always appropriate to every occasion.

Lest we forget, he was one of the key officers who protected General Ramos during the Edsa revolution 1.

And he is turning another page in his life as he faces this new challenge of irregularities in the conduct of the May 9 election.

To General Eli Rio, the Rio of #TNTrio, we salute you for braving the salvos of personal attacks and challenges thrown against you by trolls.

We greet you on your nth birthday! May you enjoy your special day with your family and friends.

Let's help him slice the cake we shall share and partake of his successes in life !

Happy birthday Sir/ General Eliseo Rio Jr!

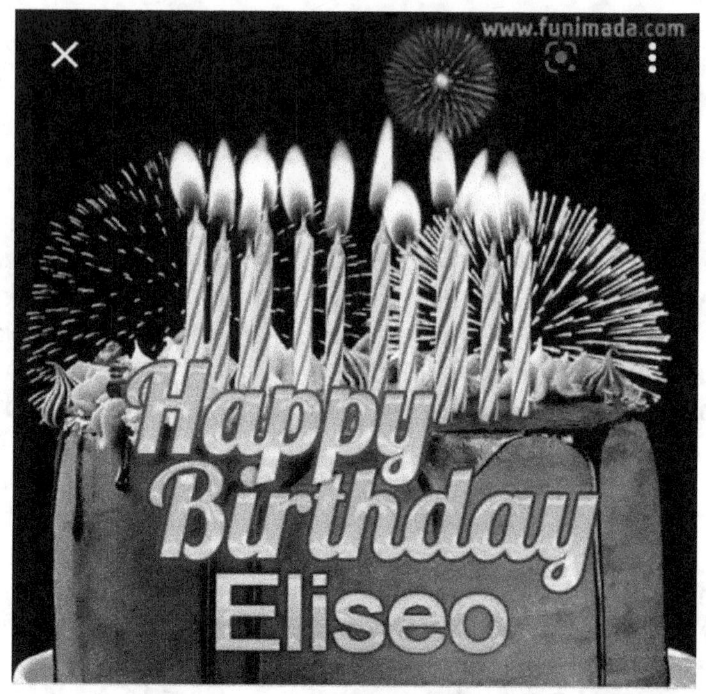

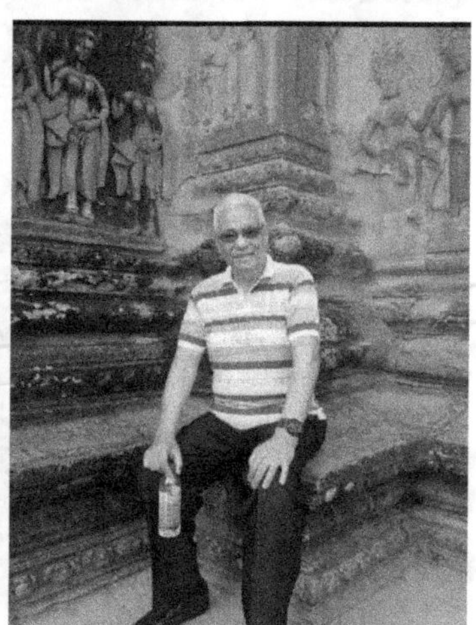

www.funimada.com
Happy
Birthday
Eliseo

COL ELISEO M RIO GSC (SC) PA
05 NOV 95 - 16 MAR 96

oooooo

26
Update – Oct. 27, 2022 –
A Question Of Law

To all,

This is to share with you revised prayer of our petition after this was reviewed by a former Justice.

Our lawyers will continue to review our petition until final filing.

During the meeting, like what I usually do when I am a complainant or respondent to a case, I play the devil's advocate.

This role enhances your case as you can discern options of what your opponent or in this case, what the SC will do to answer your prayer.

For example, questions like " Did you exhaust all administrative remedies before filing the case ?" "What is your personal interest or objective on the case ?" Are you personally being injured if your cause is not granted ?" "Why the urgent motion of your case?" Is any political party behind your case ?"Are you being funded by any political person, a candidate or a losing candidate?"

There are many more questions directed towards the petitioners motive in filing the case.

Our lawyers will be prepared for all these questions during hearing.

May the Holy Spirit provide all the answers to these questions so our cause can be heard and our prayer will be granted !

Amen.

oooooo

27
Update – Oct. 27, 2022 –
1PM, NYET – Ramblings at the top

Talks are rife about love lost between the top incumbents. Picked up this conversation from a diehard DDs. Trust is eroded already between the two as followers of the previous admin are being cleaned up from their posts and being replaced by new followers. The short honeymoon is even exhibited in one video where the incumbent ignored the presence of the once called unity. Further to this, DDs claims the incumbent is pinning the crime on the death of journalist vlogger on order of the precious admin. The last broadcast of the assassinated said if anybody wants to have him killed it would be the precious admin.

This silent war is coming out in the open as the SC justices, majority of whom were appointed by the previous admin, is reopening the tax case against the incumbent.

This DDs even whispered that the case about to be filed before the SC for the delivery of transmission logs could be favoring the previous admin who is not happy with the incumbent whom he many times called a weak leader.

The zarzuela is on. True or not, it's a Rioley's believe it or not case until it becomes an ugly war.

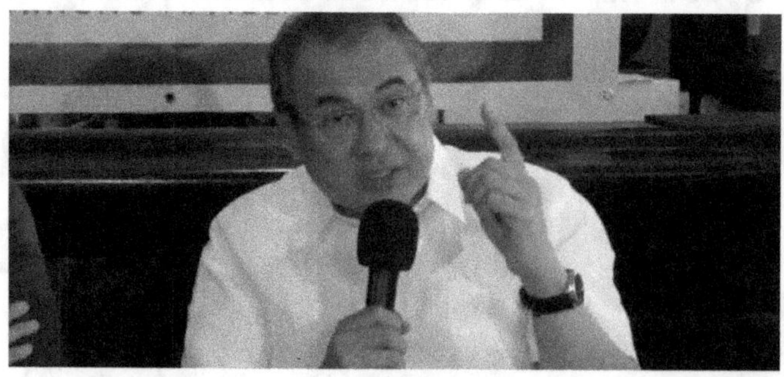

 oooooo
28
Update – October, 2022 –
Failure of Elections

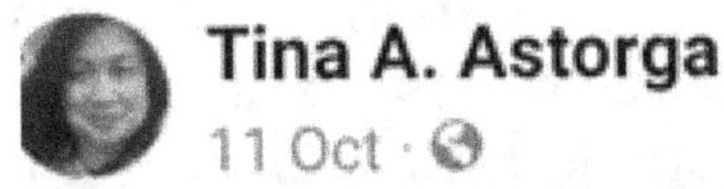

Tina A. Astorga
11 Oct · 🌐

COMELEC RED ALERT: Failure of elections must be declared. We have an illegitimate gov't ruling the nation. Based on IOM FINAL REPORT!

oooooo

29
Update – Oct. 27, 2022 –
5PM-ET – Six Days Countdown

Countdown to the moment of truth. It's six days to go and the social media is abuzz with activities on how the Thursday morning will be spent.

It will just be filing of the 100 page document asking the SC to issue TRO to telcos to save the transmission logs and to Comelec to delivery the transmission data to the court.

It's a very simple petition and we shouldn't have exercised this right at all if XXXacloba had come forward and had given us the data as early as July 15, 2022 when we sent them letters about the same request we are asking the SC.

We are sure they know we are going to the SC as this is the only recourse we have as faithful citizens who are exercising our constitutional right to know the truth behind the early result of transmission which we are questioning.

We are also moving mountains as our new team of lawyers including one brave lady lawyer who accepted our invitation to join our legal team.

As soon as we file the case before the SC, we will give copies to the press and we may have an impromptu presscon with your presence. We will wave the document and we can have selfie or groupie with all the truth warriors who we understand are coming from as far away as the north and south of Manila.

That document is not an ordinary document. Just like Moses who held the Ten Commandments before the doubting crowd of Israelites, we shall raise up high this sacred document which took us several months of painstaking sleuthing until we arrived at the moment of truth.

Thanks but no thanks to the Spox and the XXXacloba chair for strengthening our case with their disclosures and we are including them in our petition. It's a sort of damn if you do and damn if you don't case. Whatever you want to think about this happenstance, we see the hand of the Holy Spirit from the time we the #TNTrio became one and the momentum and traction came to this end.

Please don't feel rested as if we have won the case already. It's just the beginning as the case will still be heard. We need to hurdle the TRO on the telco side and there will be arguments before the SC on Comelec compliance with order from SC.

Let's all pray our petition will be granted by the SC so the whole country will know the case will either confirm or beiie the truth behind the 20M plus votes in the first hour after poll closing.

St. Jude Thaddeus whose feastday falls today, pray for us.

Amen.

Oooooo

30
Update – Oct. 27, 2022 –
11PM-ET – Finex Contest

Taking a short break today. Just flew in Cebu to conduct our annual intercollegiate finance competition where business schools participate with winners participating in the finals in Manila on November 25 at the BSP. This is held simultaneously

in Bacolod, Davao, Baguio and Pampanga where more than 50 business schools participate.

This competition was organized by my organization, Financial Executives Institute of the Philippines in 1999 as part of our advocacy for continuing education in finance. I teach in business schools also on banking and finance subjects both for college and masters programs.

For the last 20 years, because of our drive to enhance student education, we also hold finance courses for faculty in coordination with CHED.

Our efforts prove the worthiness of business and finance practical applications as many faculty themselves need upgrading with their knowledge. Since many of our Finex members are CEOs and CFOs of top companies, we envision that the future finance leaders of the country can make our country finance competitive across the globe. Many of the students and faculty pursue further studies and many of them become successful in their own fields.

During the past several years, we put emphasis now on matters of business ethics which we sorely lack in this country.

The good governance subject is already added in curriculum of business schools.

On my own, aside from regular lecture on treasury matters, I also teach bank, investment and IT scams.

By now, I include the subject of election scam as my regular feature.

We pray that unless we teach our students and faculty on proper management of business, we will become pariah of the world where corruption is more of a norm than good governance. Lately, good governance has been adopted as basic requirement for schools and companies registered with Sec, or BSP, as worldwide corruption has become more pronounced and this has been the bane to economic development of countries.

As we endeavor to clean up the mess in our election system, we shall never be able to overcome the stain of a corrupt system now taking place even in highly developed countries of the world unless we adopt a strong good governance policies both in private and public organizations.

The #TNTrio shall remain steadfast in our advocacy for good governance in government

even beyond the present case we are filing before the Supreme Court.

Let us pay attention to good governance as this is the key to the success of any business or government.

Countries that practice good governance like Singapore prove that good governance matters as foreign investments will naturally come in .

Here are snapshots of the competition in Cebu where I sat as judge with business schools from cebu, XXXaclobanXXX, bohol and XXXacloban participating.

Good luck to the winners who will compete with winners from the other sites in Manila on November 25 where top prize of P100,000 goes to the winner. Our main sponsor is JP Morgan which has been our sponsor for more than a decade already.

Oooooo

31
Update – Oct. 28, 2022 –
6AM-ET – Funding Report

To all,

We #_TNTrio would like to thank all truth warriors who helped us raise funds for the initial cost of our Supreme Court filing.

Up to this moment, we have been receiving amounts, no matter

how small or big, as your participation for this historic cause. We keep all records of receipts and disbursements and our treasurer has acknowledged all who shared until this was I to me. I will turn over all the records and amounts to her including those who sent funds to my Bdo account . We have records also of all our disbursements to our lawyers and the miscellaneous expenses like travel, food and others. All are accounted for.

We are still documenting all the receipts and disbursements from the last posting so you will all know how the funds were spent.

We shall let you know when this fund raising will end after we have filed our mandamus case.

We realize that after we file the case, we will be preparing for the big ones, meaning offense and defense lawyers, will have to be compensated by special donors.

On our part, we will also participate with our own funds and this will be recorded. We don't know how long the case will last but there are urgent motions that have to be

resolved by the Supreme Court .

As I said, the battle has not ended yet and it has just begun.

We expect a deluge of support from new donors but we want to impress upon them that there won't be political favors in the event we win the battle. We are sure there will be big exchanges in the courtroom.

While the case is on going, we enjoin all truthwarriors to keep vigil in the Supreme Court to make sure the moral support is present.

Vigilance is still our shield against undue haste in decision to be made by SC.

Meanwhile, we shall keep watch and attend all hearings and will report to you all significant developments from our case.

Oooooo

32
Update – Oct. 29, 2022 –
12AM-ET – 5 days countdown

It's five days to go and what's happening now?

Na sa printing na po kami at final na case po. Medyo Marami po 100 page per set and we will distribute them to SC, and the respondents. For press and other supporters / truth warriors we can provide soft copies either on CD or social media.

We will publish the same here in my Fb page so all truth warriors will have a chance to read our petition.

By that time, the whole country will have known our case is now in court. If our case is dismissed without any valid and acceptable reason, we bring the case to the court of public opinion.

We have already completed paying partially our lawyers acceptance fee amounting to more than 150k. This is coming from you and our personal financial support. We will pay the balance 50k as soon as we have filed our case with SC.

With your generous support, we shall be able to make things happen the way we envision how our advocacy will achieve positive results.

From day one, it was frustrating to know that we were alone on this fight for truth. Through our persistence and hard work, slowly the path became clear as the sun started to clear the fog of doubt.

Final exam na po eto and we have passed the full semester of speculations and sleuthing.

Thanks be to all the Saints and the Holy Trinity whom we invoked from day one .

Together with your prayers, we have overcome the painful challenge as we faced uncertain future of our democracy.

We will prevail po and our lawyers are real blessing po.

Maraming Maraming Salamat po sa truth warriors and we encourage you to join us this coming Thursday, November 3.

Holy Spirit, please enlighten our lawyers and also the SC to grant our petition so this country will live freely with true leaders running our beloved country.

Amen .

Eduardo Lansangan Mangune
Sana Naman ay HUWAG MAGING BULAG, PIPI at BINGI ang mga JUSTICES NATIN at HINDI maging JUSTICES NILA.

Marie Bartolome
Sharing this prayer to the Holy Spirit that we pray before all our activities and meetings in our church. May He continue to guide you and your lawyers in your quest for the truth.

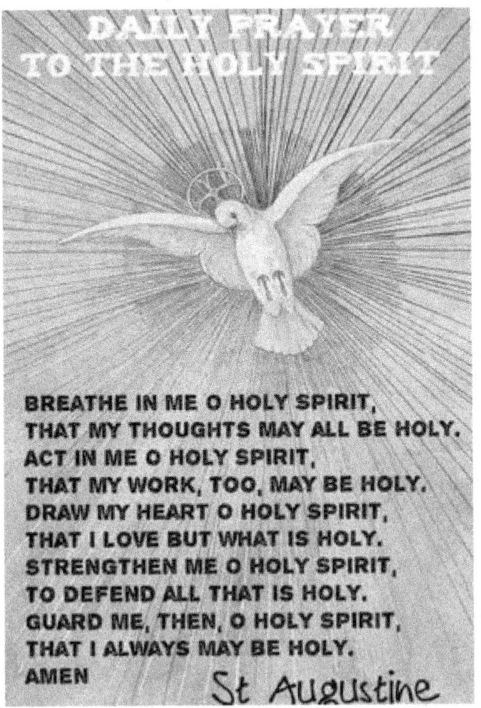

RS Grullo
The moment of truth 🙏

Lolit Teodoro
🙏Amen Amen🙏

Josephine San Jose Esteban

Patrocinia Endrinal
The truth shall prevail. Thanks to all those who helped in anyway they can in pursuing this petition. Bless all of us Lord. Amen🙏🙏🙏

Jojo V. Peñaflor
#TNTrio God bless you🙏

Loreto Salvador
May the spirit of our Lord be with you, in Jesus name Amen

Evelyn Malazarte
Amen and amen.. God bless us all 🙏🙏🙏

Ricardo Dematera
Hopefully God favors us now,amen.!!?

Meds Camba
Only "truth will set us free!"

Mercedes Dantis Lazaro
God willing, hoping for the best, for the sake of us, Filipinos 🙏

Alda Gaño
Prayers 🙏💙🌼💙🙏➤
Cherry Crisostomo
Praying for help to Mama Mary.

Maria's Life Style :" The beauty of a Senior Citizenship" ·
Follow
Amen, the spirit of the Lord be with you all
Truth warriors sa pangunguna po. Ninyo sir Franklin and TNTrio,.Thank you
Jesus for your guidance and protections to all Truth Warriors!!!

Emma Zorilla
Amen!
In your Mercy and Compassion Lord We Trust in You!

Susan Munsayac
God be with us all in this journey, and show us the path to true light.

Eppie Montes
Amen

Juses Tumamak Barte
🙏🙏🙏✨✨🙏💧💧 🕉️⚫⚫⚫🕙➤➤🟠🟠🟠❤️❤️💜🌷🌷
👆👆👆✨✨✨

Jun Pantaleon
Amen and Amen...🙏🙏🙏

Fedelina Santos
Amen 🙏🙏🙏

Marichou Peoylo Baja
🙏🙏🙏🙏🙏🙏

Melita Doronila
Amen Amen

Magdalena-Aning Pecito-Zamora Francisco

Leonardo Velasco
Amen...

Flocerfina Cruz
Amen and amen!

Magdalena-Aning Pecito-Zamora Francisco
🙏😊🏁🏁🏁🏁🏁🏁

Pau Oy Amy
Amen🙏🙏🙏🙏🙏🙏

Reynaldo Amarante
Amen🙏🙏🙏😄😄😄❤️❤️❤️❤️😄😄😄👍👍👍

Rolando Hernandez Ramos
🙏 Amen!

Josefina Magcayang
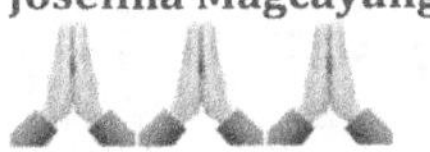

Mon F Baltazar
Amen. Godbls!

Jhun M. Malijan
🙏🙏🙏🙏🙏

Fred Santos
https://www.facebook.com/100079273802535/posts/163300449655748/?app=fbl

Elvie Lee
Prayer of Surrendering the Truth into God's Hands
Father, we are grateful that You should walk with us and strengthen us through our days. We give thanks for Your glorious world and our brothers and sisters that walk upon it. Lord, you know our hearts…
See more

Fred Santos

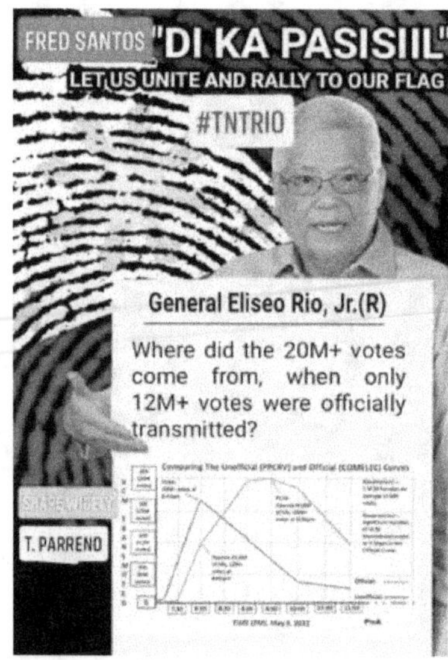

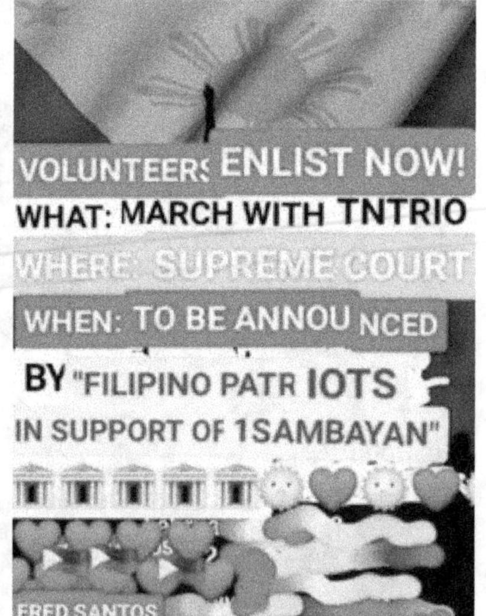

Tita Len

God the Father pls graciously hear our prayers through our Lord Jesus Christ. In His mighty name. Amen.

Christel Hazel
Thank you so much again Sir 

Trebuh Zeuqsav
SEND a copy to non-tabogo media (they're only few coz NOT FOR SALE), the UN, BBC, CNN, VOD, etc.

Eduardo Lansangan Mangune
Sana Naman ay HUWAG MAGING BULAG, PIPI at BINGI ang mga JUSTICES NATIN at HINDI maging JUSTICES NILA.

Eduardo Lansangan Mangune
Jesusa Decal dasal nalang Tayo.

Marie Bartolome
Sharing this prayer to the Holy Spirit that we pray before all our activities and meetings in our church. May He continue to guide you and your lawyers in your quest for the truth.

oooooo

33
Update – Oct. 29, 2022 –
NYET –
The TNTrio – and more prayers

A follower and truth warrior asked us how we became TNTrio. I told him when we joined forces we were pushing for truth and transparency and I coined it TNT. But that's an explosive abbreviation and I added Rio to reflect the key IT specialist on election and that's our very own General Eli Rio.

Somebody branded us three wise men after the three kings and another called us fhe holy Trinity . But I called that off because that could be blasphemous and we are just humans looking for the truth.

Now, when we challenged the election rigging, there's nobody who could challenge the automated election system except the three of us who have different but common IT backgrounds.

Gus Lagman, former comelec commisioner and Namfrel chair, recalled he was the only non lawyer commissioner and that's the problem with comelec. When automated system was passed by Congress, comelec relied solely on Smartmatic and nobody from Comelec wouldn't know how to run an automated election system and they just willingly allowed smartmatic to handle everything. So how will you know if the system is manipulated or not. No wonder even the chair nor the Spox could explain what Gus and Eli are commenting and challenging them. Gus founded the STI schools until he sold his interest to another businessman. But he is still active in Philippine computer society and other computer organizations.

General Eli is our true warrior. He is the only one who wears many hats, an electronic and electrical engineer with computer engineering background. He was NTC commissioner who straightened the anomalies in the NTC. He became DICT Usec and he had to leave the department because of political influence and he didn't approve questionable transactions there.

I am the only one who doesn't have the engineering background nor IT background. It was only accidental that after my stint in banking I dabbled in software development. After I earned my keeps from my forex trading, I invested in banking software applications because at that time banks were looking for software. I had difficulty and was losing money from my development as I got poor programmers. Then I started paying good salary to experienced programmers and I was lucky to produce some programs. Problem was I was a neophyte and I couldn't compete with stable providers. Even my own bank friends doubted my capacity whether I could deliver. Then the first product was my forte, a forex trading platform. This was in 1999. It took me a year to fully develop the prototype and my first client was BDO. For a tidy price, I accepted the challenge. Then word got around and Ibank and metrobank placed orders and my latest is east West Bank. Then more orders came along to develop software for finance companies, for investment houses, for spav companies, for trust business and many more. I basically design my own systems and I didn't have time to do programming work. I attempted to but it's so painstaking at Matiyaga. I could but I just hired the best programmers and just pay

them their dues.

Now, how did the three of us, Gus and Eli, became one force in this truth campaign. We said if no one will challenge the comelec system which is rigged with irregularities then this will happen again and again and we will just be victims. So we investigated the whole process and we were looking for the smoking gun and we found it.

That's why after six months, we became the IT investigators who never gave up and after my regular posts, suddenly I got more than 13k followers who exchanged their views with me.

Here we are now . From the number three we will soon be 3,000 then, 13,000, then 130,000, then 1,300,000, the 13,000,000, then 23,000,000 until we win the case.

That's how the good Lord built His church . A church built on trust and truth.

We assured ourselves we were doing messengerial work for the Almighty

As He has had enough of these bad leaders.

That's why we rely solely on the strength and power of the Almighty to guide us till the last moment of truth next Thursday .

oooooo

34
Update – Oct. 29 –
6PM-ET – Biding Time

To all truth warriors,

On our filing date next Thursday November 3, 2022, we will publish here the full 100 page text of our petition for TRO on the telcos and submission of data to the Court.

You may not be a lawyer to fully comprehend the text but you have to thank these brave lawyers who spent hours after hours compiling data and materials to prove our case is airtight.

Most of all, we are about to unravel the truth and the facts which the respondents cannot hide.

A truth warrior asked me what happens if the SC decides to grant our request and we are able to prove our case, I told her that the necessary action will come from our lawyers. From a simple data which will convince the SC that there were indeed irregularities, then our lawyers next move would be to right the wrong in another pleading. It's up to our lawyers to make that next move.

But what will really happen is this : the ruling will confirm our findings that there were irregularities and the respondents cannot just toss the coin and tell us to go to JCOCAE where they commanded us to go. Let the SC decide that .

This case is unprecedented and the lawyers are having hard time also in making the premises stick to the decision we want.

We don't want the SC to find grounds to dismiss our case because this is not a political matter but a matter that we voters want from a transparent election system which we didn't find in the May election.

oooooo

35
Update – Oct. 29, 2022 –
630PM-ET –
Finex Contest + Biding Time before submission

In the recently concluded intercollegiate finance competition where 50 schools participated in the elimination round, the provincial schools and universities performed very well as they dominated the competition. 16 of the 20 schools came from provincial schools in Luzon, Visayas and Mindanao and will meet in the final round which will be held in Manila on November 25, 2022.

Of the top 20 schools, three came from UP universities with UP Tacloban garnering the first, followed by UP Diliman and UP Iloilo.

What this performance shows is that our advocacy and teaching module upgrades have helped provincial schools improve the quality of education. Students don't have to come to Manila to top board exams in accounting, engineering, medicine and other fields.

My organization, Finex, continues to provide higher education training both for students and faculty. Our members contribute their time and effort to give lectures to these provincial schools so they won't be left out of the many developments in the finance world.

While in Cebu, a university invited me to give face to face lecture on treasury management and my favorite subject which is Lessons from bank, investment and IT scams. They also want to know more about dangers of investing in crypto currency. I offered my services pro Bono but they have to take care of the necessities.

But I told them I can do this only after we have won our mandamus case before the SC.

Strangely, of my 13,000 followers, many of the faculty and students have been following my posts and they are praying with us so political stability with leaders chosen by the people not by automated system should be leading the country .

Meanwhile, back in Manila, #TNTrio are finalizing details of the Thursday filing.

We have standby plans on how to make sure the SC will take up the TRO ahead of the November 9 deadline by telcos.

To all our truth warriors who have organized themselves to join us next Thursday, we would to thank you for taking your time out and spending it with us. Just a piece of advice, we should be following city rules on mass gathering and let's make sure there won't be infiltrators who will cause some alarms. Guard your ranks and don't break them and let's tell the whole country and the world we are one in our claim for honest, clean and credible election. No more to election rigging as we don't want non winners to hold higher offices in our beloved country.

oooooo

36
Update – Oct. 29, 2022 –
Poster – Rally (Poster)

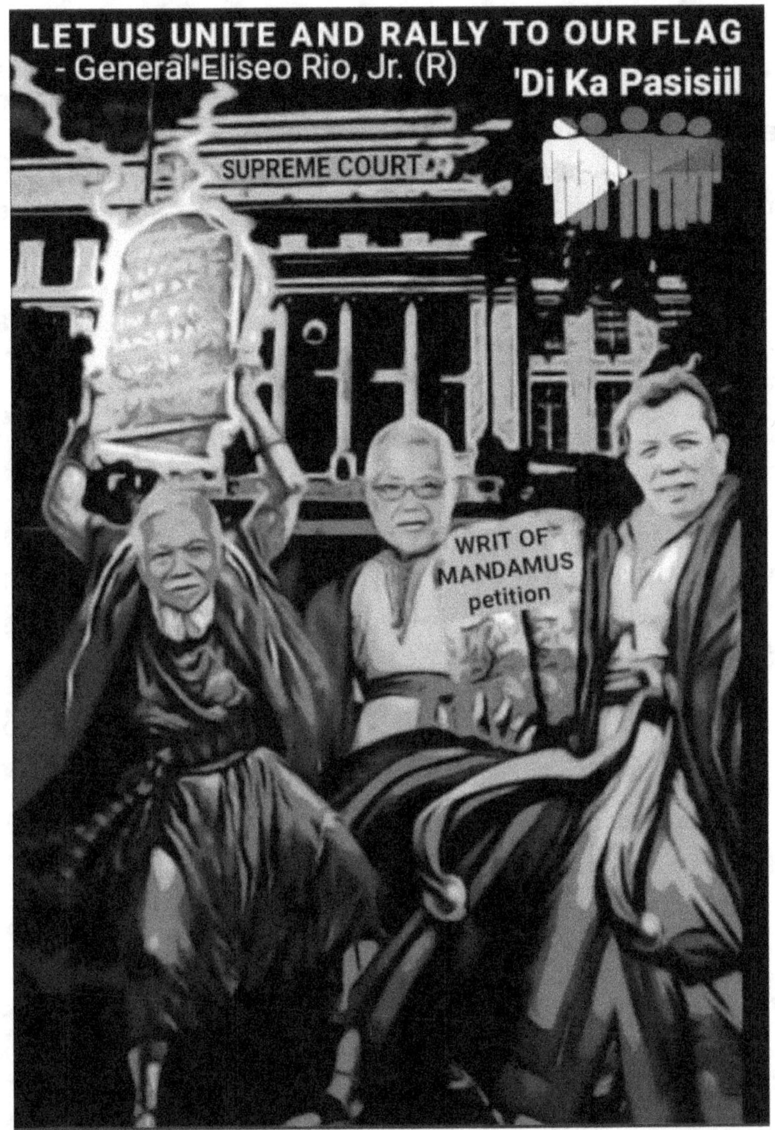

ooooooo

37
Update – Oct. 30, 2022 –
NYET –
Waiting and Funding news

A friend follower and truth warrior sent me his contribution to our legal fund. Unfortunately, nag error kasi exceeded limit na rin gcash ko.

Our treasurer po will have her gcash restored by tomorrow or first day of November . And will give her record of all contributions so she can reconcile all donations.

By Thursday, we would have given already what is due the signatory and the associates who completed the petition.

The next round will be for litigation fund . We #TNTrio will share in this fund naman.

Let's pray that we will be able to sustain the litigation which may take some time. We are looking at 2 to 3 months before decision is made by SC. But the TROnon telco is urgent and we will follow this up after we file the case this Thursday po.

Will see you this Thursday . Yung Hindi maka punta post namin po full text ng petition dito Sa fb so you can read the petition.

Maraming Maraming Salamat po.
#TNTrio

oooooo

38
Update – October 30, 2022 –
NY-ET –
Nearing date of Petition to Supreme Court

It's Monday, October 31, last day of the month. And it's just 3 days to go till November 3, our filing date.

If you want to join the truth warriors who will be there, kindly observe some important reminders :

1. This is not a rally. This is just an expression of support for our mandamus and tro petition.

2. Avoid wearing colors of political parties to avoid being branded as supporters of political candidates. Preferably west white or black.

3. Bring umbrellas just in case.

4. Snacks will be provided.

5. Streets should be kept free from traffic.

6. No loudspeakers or no noise whatsoever so as not to invite crowd control.

7. The #TNTrio will be available for selfies or groupies to those who want to have memoirs of the historic petition day as early as 9 am.

8. Crowds may stay on sidewalks outside the SC gate.

9. Target time of filing is 10am and only petitioners will be allowed inside SC.

10. After filing, the petitioners May hold impromptu presscon with justice reporters. They will be given press kit so they can publish the event in their papers.

11. The petitioners, the #TNTrio will step outside the SC gates for photo op with truthwarriors raising the received copy of petition. Such photos can be shared in your social media to tell the country and the world that we will never allow cheating in last May election and future elections to keep integrity, honesty, transparency, credibility in our election system minus smartmatic system .

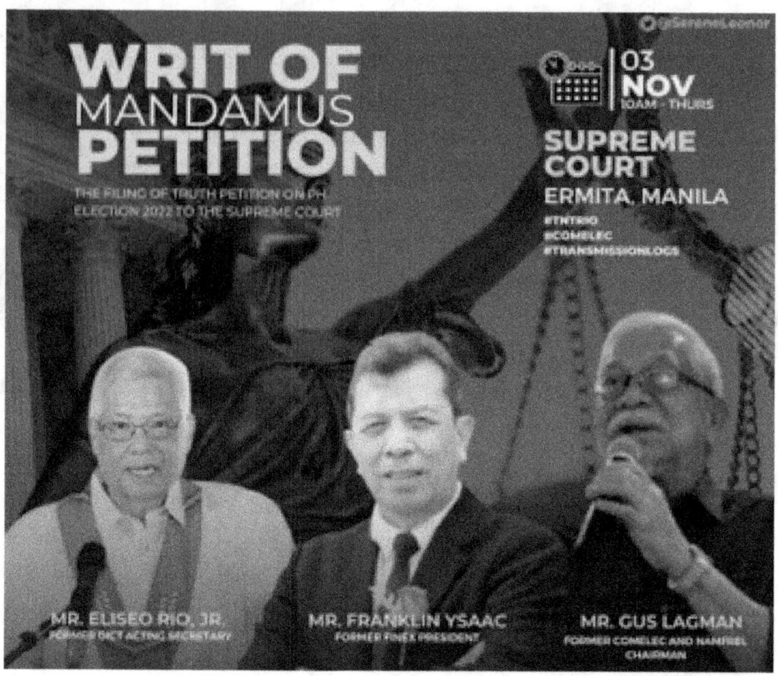

oooooo

39
Update – Oct. 30, 2022 –
3PM, NYET – Eliseo Rio Jr. Explanation

In response to many queries about possible setbacks or drawbacks from our petition, we already wrote about this and let me reiterate our response:

1. If TRO on telcos is not granted, we are still keeping our cards that the main course is for Comelec to disclose the transmission reports during the first hour as this is the critical moment where Comelec claims 21M was counted in favor of the incumbents. Our very own General Eli Rio has already presented the questionable data and the comelec posting of the graph leads to Comelec's admission there were no 21M votes counted in the first hour but only 12M. Please read General Rio's

explanation. The tro on telco is only for preservation of data just in case Comelec refuses to grant our request before SC.

2. To suggestion we share this petition with foreign media, we will definitely share this with them to tell the whole world the May election is fraught with frauds.

3. To query that the SC may not grant our petition even if our petition is not even political, we will make it known to all that such dismissal only means SC doesn't recognize our constitutional right and it violates our right under freedom of information act. When this happens, then this will be another travesty of Justice.

We don't see SC will not grant our petition as it will not do harm to persons but our petition is a very simple petition and there is no other motive except to ask Comelec to validate that there were transmissions made during the first hour. That's all. Whatever repercussions this petition will bring if Comelec doesn't grant or grants our request, this is not our immediate concern. It's up to our lawyers to do the necessary to extract the truth .

Here is General Rio's explanation of the irregularities of the May election.

Even if COMELEC did not give us the transmission logs on the first two hours (7pm to 9pm) after voting closed on May 9 that we were asking for since July 15, 2022, to show the observed irregularities that the Transparency Server Is updating the public, a breakthrough occurred when COMELEC showed the "Accumulated VCM Transmissions" graph (Pic3) in a Forum on October 18, where COMELEC Chairman George Garcia was the Guest of Honor. That graph was shown to prove that there was no irregularities in the 2022 VCM transmissions because this just jibed with the transmissions done on the 2010, 2013, 2016 and 2019 automated elections.

But looking closely at the VCM transmission graph, one will immediately notice that the transmissions in the 2022 election peaked two (2) hours after the transmission started, in stark contrast

3:31
◀ Viber

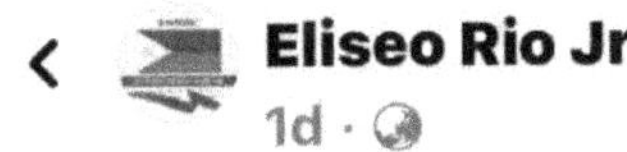

‹   **Eliseo Rio Jr**   **...**
1d · 🌐

with the counting of the Transparency Server that PEAKED just an hour after voting closed at 7pm, May 9, 2022. This is a clear discrepancy on the counting results shown in the first two hours where the VOTES COUNTED BY THE TRANSPARENCY SERVER WERE HIGHER THAN THE VOTES BEING ACTUALLY OFFICIALLY TRANSMITTED BY THE VCMs.

We would agree with COMEEC that there were no irregularities in the VCM transmissions as depicted in their "Accomulated VCM Transmission" graph. It is the first two hours reports of the Transparency Server that were highly irregular! It seems that the Transparency Server was conditioning the minds of the public as to what the official results will be, because in its first hour update of an unbelievable PEAK of 20M+ votes shown at 8:02pm, "tapos na ang boksing" as to who won the Presidency and VP. Where

 **Write a comment...**     

Home   Friends   Marketplace   Feeds   Notifications   Menu

did that 20M+ votes come from, when at that time, the accumulated VCM transmissions were only about 12M+ votes?

COMELEC must explain this discrepancy to public by showing the actual time VCM transmissions started on May 9, 2022, as shown in COMELEC's "Accumulated VCM Transmissions", corroborated by the telcos' Call Detail Records (CDRs). COMELEC must also demonstrate to the public the actual time needed to print eight (8) copies of the precinct Election Result (ER).

The COMELEC can no longer use the excuse that these simple requests require voluminous data, for it will be only seen as delaying tactics.

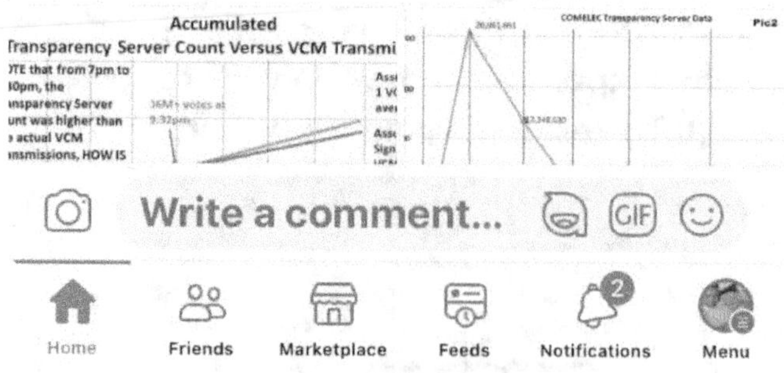

Result (ER).

The COMELEC can no longer use the excuse that these simple requests require voluminous data, for it will be only seen as delaying tactics.

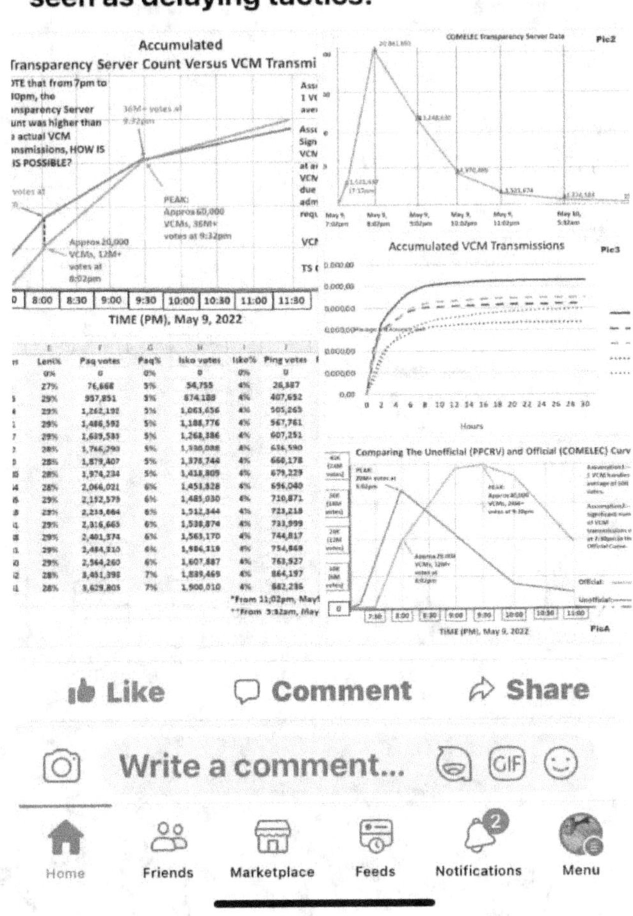

👍 Like   💬 Comment   ↪ Share

Write a comment...

Home   Friends   Marketplace   Feeds   Notifications   Menu

oooooo

40
Update, October 2022 –
Poster

oooooo

41
Update – Oct. 31, 2022 –
8AM-NYET – Truth Must Prevail

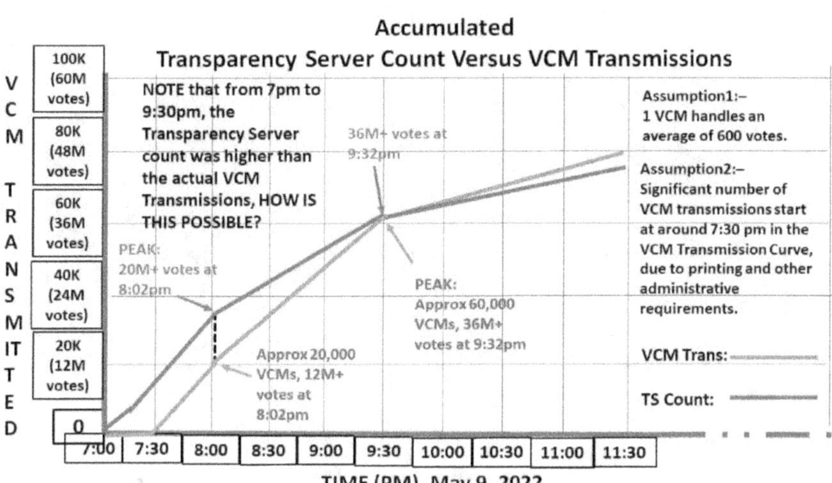

Date/Time	BBM votes	BBM%	Leni votes	Leni%	Paq votes	Paq%	Isko votes	Isko%	Ping votes	Ping%	Total	Hourly #Votes	From/To
May 9/7:03pm	0	0%	0	0%	0	0%	0	0%	0	0%	0	0	
May 9/7:17pm	958,219	63%	409,608	27%	76,668	5%	54,755	4%	26,387	2%	1,525,637		
May 9/8:02pm	12,065,875	60%	5,756,125	29%	957,851	5%	874,188	4%	407,652	2%	20,061,691	20,061,691	7:02pm/8:02pm
May9/8:17pm	15,339,876	60%	7,268,834	29%	1,262,192	5%	1,063,656	4%	505,265	2%	25,455,825		
May9/8:32pm	17,541,799	60%	8,311,501	29%	1,486,592	5%	1,188,776	4%	567,761	2%	29,096,429		
May9/8:47pm	18,975,119	60%	8,979,607	29%	1,639,535	5%	1,268,386	4%	607,251	2%	31,469,898		
May9/9:02pm	20,084,651	60%	9,493,702	28%	1,766,790	5%	1,330,088	4%	636,590	2%	33,310,321	13,248,630	8:02pm/9:02pm
May9/9:17pm	20,978,088	60%	9,921,820	28%	1,879,407	5%	1,378,744	4%	660,178	2%	34,818,232		
May9/9:32pm	21,725,982	60%	10,282,280	28%	1,974,234	5%	1,418,809	4%	679,229	2%	36,080,534		
May9/9:47pm	22,410,199	60%	10,613,144	28%	2,066,021	6%	1,451,828	4%	696,040	2%	37,239,232		
May9/10:02pm	23,017,285	60%	10,915,045	29%	2,152,579	6%	1,485,030	4%	710,871	2%	38,280,810	4,970,489	9:02pm/10:02pm
May9/10:17pm	23,552,108	60%	11,183,118	29%	2,235,664	6%	1,511,344	4%	723,213	2%	39,204,447		
May9/10:32pm	24,070,851	60%	11,447,751	29%	2,316,665	6%	1,533,874	4%	733,999	2%	40,108,140		
May9/10:47pm	24,565,511	60%	11,691,138	29%	2,401,374	6%	1,561,170	4%	744,817	2%	40,966,010		
May9/11:02pm	25,051,855	60%	11,925,131	29%	2,484,310	6%	1,586,319	4%	754,869	2%	41,802,484	3,521,674	10:02pm/11:02pm
May9/11:17pm	25,489,420	60%	12,145,860	29%	2,564,260	6%	1,607,887	4%	761,927	2%	42,571,354		
May10/5:32am	30,228,129	60%	14,400,852	28%	3,451,398	7%	1,839,469	4%	864,197	2%	50,778,545	1,374,588	*
May11/3:18pm	31,164,175	59%	14,822,051	28%	3,629,805	7%	1,900,010	4%	851,236	2%	52,338,277	19,077	**

*From 11:02pm, May9 to 5:32am, May10 (Average per hour for 6.53 hours)

**From 5:32am, May10 to 3:18pm, May11 (Average per hour for 81.76 hours)

Pic1

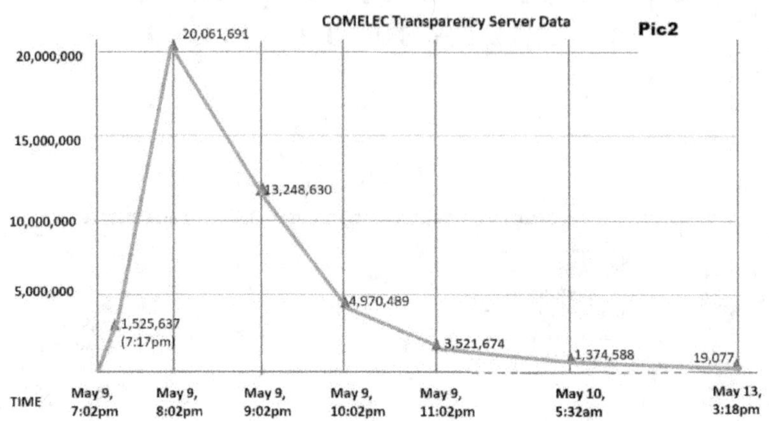

COMELEC Transparency Server Data
Pic2
20,061,691
13,248,630
4,970,489
3,521,674
1,374,588
19,077
1,525,637
(7:17pm)
20,000,000
15,000,000
10,000,000
5,000,000
TIME
May 9, 7:02pm
May 9, 8:02pm
May 9, 9:02pm
May 9, 10:02pm
May 9, 11:02pm
May 10, 5:32am
May 13, 3:18pm

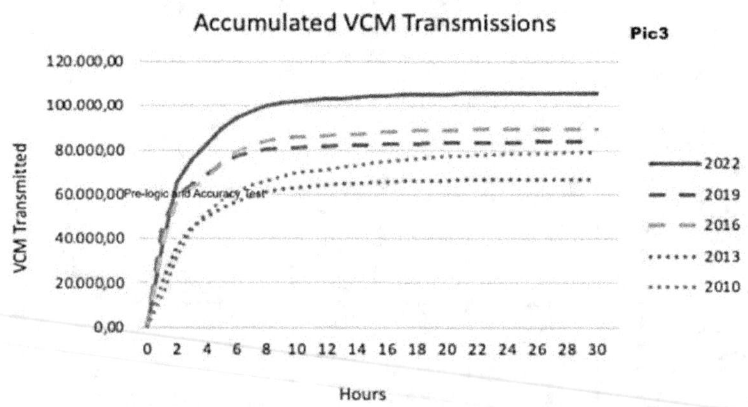

Accumulated VCM Transmissions
Pic3
120.000,00
100.000,00
80.000,00
60.000,00
40.000,00
20.000,00
0,00
VCM Transmitted
Pre-logic and Accuracy Test
0 2 4 6 8 10 12 14 16 18 20 22 24 26 28 30
Hours
2022
2019
2016
2013
2010

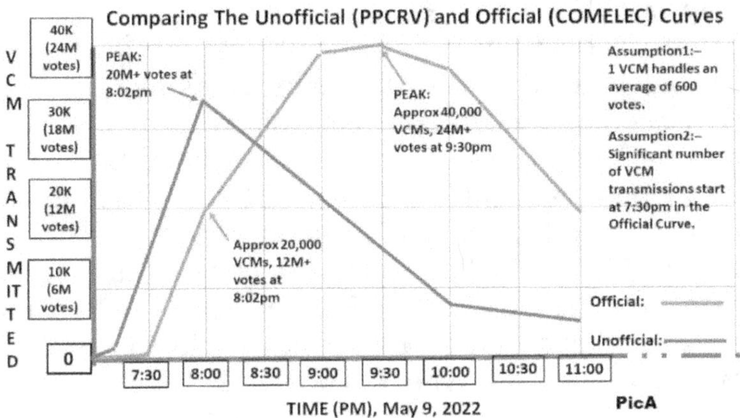

By Eliseo Rio Jr

Even if COMELEC did not give us the transmission logs on the first two hours (7pm to 9pm) after voting closed on May 9 that we were asking for since July 15, 2022, to show the observed irregularities that the Transparency Server Is updating the public, a breakthrough occurred when COMELEC showed the "Accumulated VCM Transmissions" graph (Pic3) in a Forum on October 18, where COMELEC Chairman George Garcia was the Guest of Honor. That graph was shown to prove that there was no irregularities in the 2022 VCM transmissions because this just jibed with the transmissions done on the 2010, 2013, 2016 and 2019 automated elections.

But looking closely at the VCM transmission graph, one will immediately notice that the transmissions in the 2022 election peaked two (2) hours after the transmission started, in stark contrast with the counting of the Transparency Server that PEAKED just an hour after voting closed at 7pm, May 9, 2022. This is a clear discrepancy on the counting results shown in the first two hours where the VOTES COUNTED BY THE

TRANSPARENCY SERVER WERE HIGHER THAN THE VOTES BEING ACTUALLY OFFICIALLY TRANSMITTED BY THE VCMs.

We would agree with COMEEC that there were no irregularities in the VCM transmissions as depicted in their "Accomulated VCM Transmission" graph. It is the first two hours reports of the Transparency Server that were highly irregular! It seems that the Transparency Server was conditioning the minds of the public as to what the official results will be, because in its first hour update of an unbelievable PEAK of 20M+ votes shown at 8:02pm, "tapos na ang boksing" as to who won the Presidency and VP. Where did that 20M+ votes come from, when at that time, the accumulated VCM transmissions were only about 12M+ votes?

COMELEC must explain this discrepancy to public by showing the actual time VCM transmissions started on May 9, 2022, as shown in COMELEC's "Accumulated VCM Transmissions", corroborated by the telcos' Call Detail Records (CDRs). COMELEC must also demonstrate to the public the actual time needed to print eight (😎 copies of the precinct Election Result (ER).

The COMELEC can no longer use the excuse that these simple requests require voluminous data, for it will be only seen as delaying tactics.

oooooo

42
Update – Oct. 31, 2022 –
10AM-NYET –
Intervension Lawyers

Today, I feel good that we receive offers from lawyers who will assist us and they will file as intervention lawyers.

What's the good thing about intervention lawyers. On their own, they will cite our case and will act on their own as litigation lawyers.

What happens is this, the more intervention lawyers we have the more we have lawyers who can litigate before the SC even if they are not part of our legal team.

This is good news for our case .

If there are more lawyers going to help us as intervention lawyers, the stronger our case will be.

Maraming Salamat po sa mga volunteer intervention lawyers.

God has answered our prayers by sending these brave lawyers to us.

Holy Spirit, please continue to solicit assistance from more intervention lawyers including lawyers of other candidates.

Amen.

oooooo

43
Update – Oct. 31, 2022 –
2PM-NYET – Posters

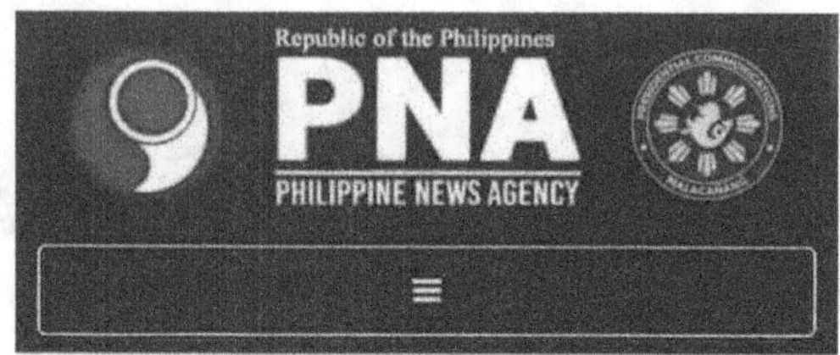

Comelec deletes files from servers used in May polls

By Ferdinand Patinio

June 15, 2022, 6:04 pm

oooooo

44
Update – Oct. 31, 2022 –
12Noon-NYET - More posters

Franklin Ysaac
7h · 🌐

To organizers of this Thursday event, we wish to remind you to police your ranks.

We were advised there will be marshals appointed to make sure the crowd is safe from any potential infiltration by bad elements.

We sought assistance from our very own General Eli Rio who used to be head of ISAFP and who has had experience in crowd control during edsa revolution and he assured us and everyone, there will be support from retired personnel in his former organization just like the same support his team provided us during our first presscon last June 2, 2022.

Nevertheless, as the saying goes, to be forewarned is to be forearmed not literally.

We are followers of truth and we will not allow any untoward element to disturb our peaceful assembly.

St. Michael the Archangel, please protect us from harm or from evil people this Thursday.

Amen.

COUNTDOWN BEGINS FOR THIS HISTORIC FILING OF MANDAMUS

What: Filing of Mandamus
Where: Supreme Court
When: November 3, 2022
Time: 10:00am

pls join us in this historic day of the filing of Mandamus with SC.

Wear black or white please..

Thank you!

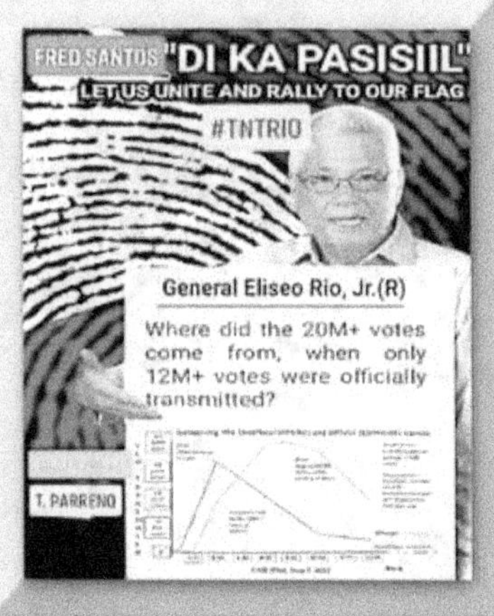

Accumulated
Transparency Server Count Versus VCM Transmissions
VCM TRANSMITTED
100K
(60M votes)
80K
(48M votes)
60K
(36M votes)
40K
(24M votes)
20K
(12M votes)
0
NOTE that from 7pm to 9:30pm, the Transparency Server count was higher than the actual VCM Transmissions, HOW IS THIS POSSIBLE?
36M+ votes at 9:32pm
Assumption1:–
1 VCM handles an average of 600 votes.
Assumption2:–
Significant number of VCM transmissions start at around 7:30 pm in the VCM Transmission Curve, due to printing and other administrative requirements.
PEAK:
20M+ votes at 8:02pm
PEAK:
Approx 60,000 VCMs, 36M+ votes at 9:32pm
Approx 20,000 VCMs, 12M+ votes at 8:02pm
VCM Trans:
TS Count:
7:00 7:30 8:00 8:30 9:00 9:30 10:00 10:30 11:00 11:30
TIME (PM), May 9, 2022
@SereneLeonor
WRIT OF MANDAMUS PETITION
THE FILING OF TRUTH PETITION ON PH ELECTION 2022 TO THE SUPREME COURT
03 NOV
10AM – THURS
SUPREME COURT
ERMITA, MANILA
#TNTRIO
#COMELEC
#TRANSMISSIONLOGS
MR. ELISEO RIO, JR.
FORMER DICT ACTING SECRETARY
MR. FRANKLIN YSAAC
FORMER FINEX PRESIDENT
MR. GUS LAGMAN
FORMER COMELEC AND NAMFREL CHAIRMAN

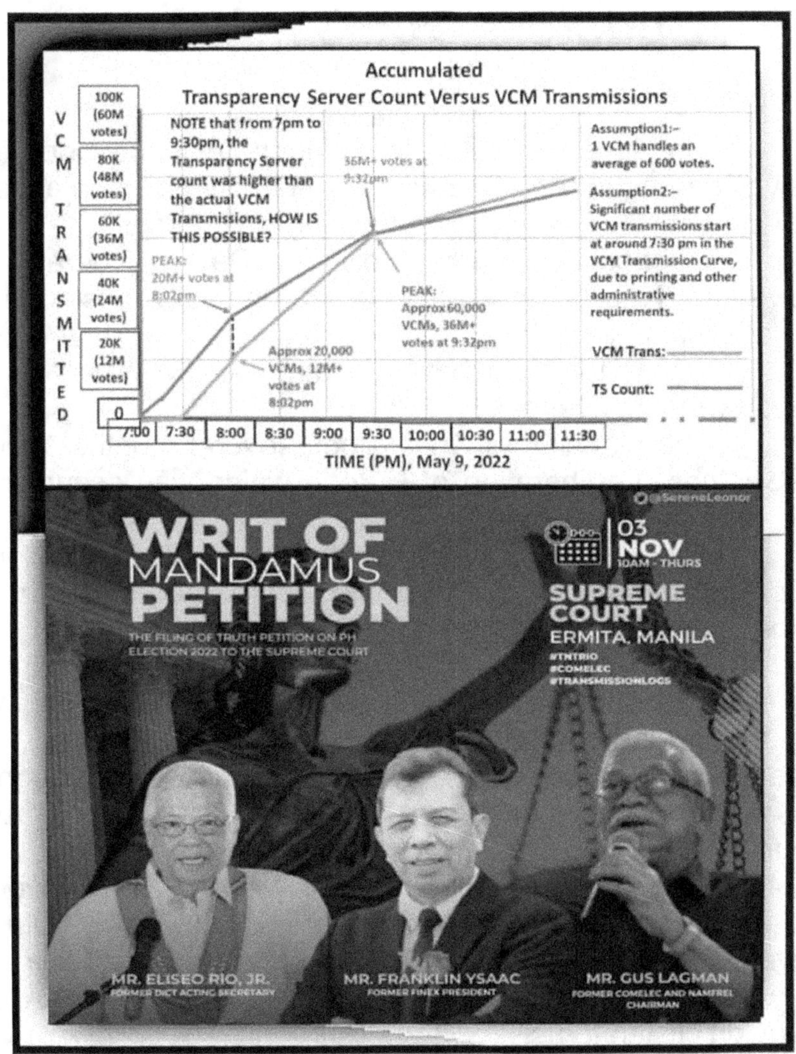

ooooooo

45
Update = Oct. 31, 2022 –
2PM – NYET
Truth will win

On June 6, 1944, the biggest Allied seaborne Invasion began with thousands of soldiers, ships, planes landing in Normandy coast attacking Nazi forces.

Dubbed D-Day or simply The Day or Operation Overlord, Nazi Germany fell after the massive onslaught of allied forces.

It was the fight between good and evil with the good winning over evil.

The planning of D-Day took several months after US joined the liberation of Europe which was occupied by Nazi Germans for many years.

Today, it's D-Day minus One, where D stands for Democracy and we will dub this Operation Mandamus. The operation plan will be revealed tomorrow.

From the deafening loss of democracy the evening of May 9, 2022, the forces of good beginning with one lone campaigner, the number grew to three. It was a campaign that was claimed to be a loss campaign as we didn't have evidence to prove the numbers were numbing, so overwhelming that people lost the will to fight. We didn't give up. We never wavered. We never lost our faith. We fought in every corner for the truth, even if the media didn't want to cover us. Not even lawyers then would dare touch us and the church wouldn't listen to us.

As the moment of truth became known to all, truth supporters whom we called warriors became the new force of good fighting the force of evil.

Tomorrow is the Deus ex Machina , the Day of Mandamus where truth will be revealed.

Let the forces of good come into the open and the forces of evil will be crushed.

May the Power of the Almighty save us just like the power of the recitation of the Most Holy Rosary saved Christian world from the invaders of Christianity.

Amen.

oooooo

46
Update – Nov. 1, 2022 –
7PM-NYET –
Purgatory

Today, November 2, Christians all over the world commemorate all souls in purgatory. That is the place or state in which the souls who died in venial sins or who have fully stoned for their past transgressions, are purified before entering paradise. The suffering of purgatory consists of intense pain of longing for God, whose beatific vision is delayed. Paradise and hell are eternal, while purgatory will end at the judgement day. We can help the souls in purgatory expiate their sins by offering Alma, prayers and Masses.

The proof of the existence of purgatory is in the 2nd book of Maccabees. It says that Judas Maccabaeus offered prayers at the temple of Jerusalem for those who had died while wearing the amulets of the idols. They could not go to paradise, because they died in sun; neither they could go to hell, because they were fighting a holy war for Yahweh. Therefore, they went into a place for purification, which we call purgatory. As Scripture says: He made atonement for the dead that they might be freed from their sins (2 Maccabees 12: 46).

Let's all pray for the souls of our departed family members, friends, relatives.

I am always praying for my parents, brother and sister who have joined our parents. I am also praying for my classmates and my close friends who lost their lives to Covid .

I am praying for victims of Ejk and murder of journalists so they will find peace in the Lord.

Lastly, I am praying for the murderers, plunderers, and the ones who committed the sin of stealing our democracy by rigging the May 9 election. It's not too late. God is waiting for you to return the monies you stole and to ask forgiveness for your crimes against humanity and for rigging the May 9 election.

May God be our refuge during this special day for the souls who are waiting for our prayers.

Amen.

oooooo

47
Update – Nov. 2, 2022 –
4PM-NYET –
Instructions to the Public

TNtrio Supreme Court Mandamus (TSCM) Update Nov 1,2022.

Important Please Take note.. We dont attend a rally but a show of support to the filing of the Mandamus by the TNtrio.. ________________________________

What TNTrio Filing of Mandamus

Where Supreme Court, Padre Faura, Manila City

When Nov 3, 2022 10am Attire Black or white tops (Blouse or Tshirt)

____

Details:

8am Holy Rosary 9am Arrival of TNTrio Parking Meet/ see Supporters Photo Shoot

9:50am TNtrio will proceed inside Supreme Court

10 am Filing of Mandamus 10 am Holy Mass (confirmed)

*After the mass: Serving of Snacks

*After the Filing TNTrio interview w/ Media Meet/ see supporters Photo shoot with the filed Mandamus to show the whole world the very first challenge to the May 9, 2022 election. ________________________________

Scenario: If the attendees will count 200 and more , it is not advisable to assemble at the venue before the time of 8am... Suggested Assembly areas before 8 am. But Derecho na sa venue if you arrive at past 8am .

* Salamanca Plaza Olivia Kalaw cor Taft ave after LUNETA from Lawton UN LRT Station (for everone

coming from caloocan, QC . Babaan ng LLRT Station-UN)

* Jollibee Kalaw street accross Maria Orosa Street

* Robinson's

*Pedro Gil cor Escoda Street Philippine Independent National Cathedral

Hindi magmarch or gropo ang magsabay. By 2's or 3's, may mauna tapus may nasunod, normal na lakad hanggang matapus, papuntang Padre Faura...

*Galing Salamanca, baybayin ang taft avenue kanan sa Padre Faura..Pagdating sa harap ng SC, maglinya isang file nakatalikud sa SC Building...along the pathway...

Ang galing sa Jollibee Kalaw, maglakad towards Maria Orosa Street kaliwa siya sa Padre faura. Pagdating sa SC harap, form a single line behind the first line, see to it nasa gitna siya sa naunang dalawa sa harap niya and so forth and so on.

Ang galing Robinsons, Kanan sa Padre Faura, magform din ng single line along the Faura street by the pathway, facing the Supreme Court.

Ang galing sa Pedro Gil, lakad along Taft avenue kaliwa sa Padre Faura, ang form a single line behind the first line..See to it nasa gitna ng dalawa sa harap...and so forth and so on. We do so to prevent anyone to cross roads to and fro anytime..the area is busy and one way street. May Social distancing. Please leave a space for the pedestrian behind the second single line... sa parehong hanay ...yong nakatalikud sa SC at sa tapat nakaharap sa SC. Hindi rin sa kalsada ng Padre Faura..Busy ang road na iyan at one way pa kaya need mag ingat talaga. Strict reminder:

*Wear your face mask all the time.

* Social distancing. * please wear black or white tops (blouse or tshirt)

* Bring umbrella or rain coat

* Bring extra Tshirt

* No extra commotion , head towards the venue peacefully. silently..wala lang, may puntahan lang. * will not cause obstruction ng pedestrian. nor cause or obstruct traffic

* Clean as you go..No loitering pls. * No chanting * No placards * After filing, on the second photo shoot with the TNTrio, with the filed Mandamus, those lining the pathway facing the Supreme Court, may now cross Padre Faura carefully...join the other side, and find your place for the group picture taking, facing back supreme court building. Or with the Supreme court Building as the Background.

* Marshalls shall be assigned 4 on one side and another 4 on the other.

*Mag ingat ang lahat. know everyone beside you.

* Good luck! God bless..! * Mabuhay!!!!!

History Unfolds Tomorrow Nov 3 at the Supreme Court. The filing of petition for MANDAMUS by the #TNTrio See u there!

oooooo

48
Update – Nov. 3, 2022 –
9AM – NYET –
Day of filing Petition to SC

The day began with Mass celebrated by the running priest, Fr. Robert Reyes, who blessed our petition folders, which we filed after the Mass.

Thanks be to the Lord, the weather was sunny and friendly. There was police presence and after General Eli Rio introduced himself, the police was cooperative and did not attempt to disperse the crowd. The crowd, mostly truth warriors, found time to bond with the #TNTrio, and did selfies and groupies.

These photos are testament to the support by truth warriors who came from nearby towns and provinces outside Manila.

We were overwhelmed by the presence of truth warriors and we are proud to share these photos as memento of this beautiful occasion where hopes have come alive after six months of sulking from election fiasco.

This day of filing is a product of six months research and sleuthing until we found hard evidence re election irregularities.

Petition
for
WRIT OF
MANDAMUS
#TNTrio
- Eliseo Rio, Jr
- Franklin Ysaac
- Gus Lagman
...ngayun pa lang nila
mararamdaman na may
nakikipaglaban pa rin
para sa katotohanan,
mabuhay!
at salamat po sa Inyo!!

oooooo

49
Update – Nov. 3, 2022
2PM – NYET – Supreme Court – Abogado.com,ph

Nov 3, 2022 @ 15:31

SC urged to require

Comelec, Smartmatic to

preserve digital records

of 2022 polls

🔒 abogado.com.ph

oooooo

50
Update – Nov. 3, 2022 –
4PM – NYET – Media coverage

Instead, I pursued an MBA degree at Ateneo and joined Citibank which was then called FNCB. Hence, I became a banker but I studied banking laws on my own and I teach banking laws together with finance subject in schools and other fora and I became consultant to many banks. But I am more of an IT where I developed many bank software and installed them with many banks.

That's how I became one of the originals of #TNTrio. This was shared with me yesterday. GMA as well as other networks have covered our SC filing . Now we are in the mainstream media whereas before we were left out in the cold after we held two presscon.

Since this is special news, there will be more coverage if and when TRO is issued next week hopefully before the November 9 deadline.

But what's conspicuous in this GMA news is it incorrectly mentioned my name as lawyer Ysaac. The other networks identified me as software app developer which is correct.

My further comment is this. I mentioned here that after my graduation from foreign service course in UP, I wanted to study law in UP as I joined UP college of law fratenity, Alpha Phi Beta fraternity. But after the tumultuous period before martial law where I was very active in demos against the dictator and I was a councilor in the UP Arts and Sciences Student Council, my mother didn't encourage me to pursue law

ooooooo

51
Update – Nov. 3, 2022
6PM – NYET –
Here's part 22 of our petition.

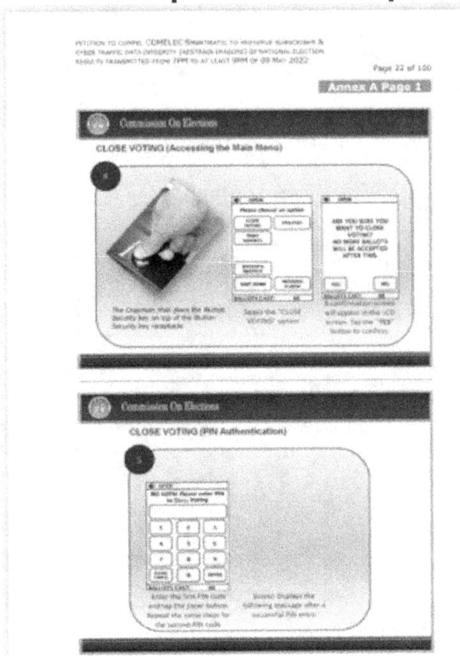

VERIFICATION
SWORN CERTIFICATION AGAINST FORUM SHOPPING
AFFIDAVIT OF SERVICE
VERIFICATION FOR EFFICIENT USE OF PAPER RULE

We: Eliseo Mijares Rio (Filipino of legal age with residence at Lot 7 Block 11 Soldiers Hill -
Barangay Putatan 1772 Muntinlupa City)
Augosto Cadeliña Lagman (Filipino of legal age with residence at 6093 Palm Street -
Poblacion 1210 Makati City)
Franklin Fayloga Ysaac (Filipino of legal age with residence at 2210 Beacon
Condominium - Chino Roces Avenue - Legaspi Village 1223 Makati City)

hereby **verify** that we have read this petition and that the same is true to the best of our own
personal knowledge. We **certify** that:

(a)   We have not theretofore commenced any other action or proceeding involving the
same issues in the Supreme Court, Court of Appeals, or any other tribunal or agency.

(b)   To the best of our own personal knowledge, there is no other similar action pending in
the Supreme Court, Court of Appeals, or any other tribunal or agency.

(c)   If there is any action or proceeding which is either pending or may have been
terminated, we shall state the status thereof.

(d)   If we thereafter learn that a similar action or proceeding is pending before the Supreme
Court, the Court of Appeals, or any other tribunal or agency, we undertake to report
that fact within 5 days therefrom to this Honorable Supreme Court.

We respectfully comply with Rule 13 Section 17 by attesting that copies of this petition will
be sent by courier (instead of personal service) to [below] because of time constraints.

Commission on Elections	8/F Palacio del Gobernador Andres Soriano corner General Luna Intramuros 1002 Manila
Smartmatic Total Information Management	Unit 2206 22/F The Trade and Financial Tower 7th Avenue corner 32nd Street Bonifacio Global City 1634 Taguig
DITO Tele Community	DITO CME Holdings President Ernest R. Alberto 21st Floor UGENNA Tower Rizal Drive corner 4th Avenue Bonifacio Global City 1634 Taguig
Globe Telecom	Globe Telecom President Ernest L. Cu Globe Tower @ 2nd Street corner 7th Avenue Bonifacio Global City 1634 Taguig
Smart Communications	Smart Communications President Alfredo S. Panlilio Ramon Cojuangco Building Makati Avenue corner Ayala Avenue Legaspi Village 1200 Makati City

Efficient use of paper rule: We verify that electronic copies of this petition in PORTABLE
DOCUMENT FORMAT (PDF) in non-editable optical COMPACT DISC (CD) media will be sent to the
above. Please see in Page 100 the postal registry receipts and/or proof of courier service.

ELISEO MIJARES RIO Junior   AUGOSTO CADELIÑA LAGMAN

FRANKLIN FAYLOGA YSAAC

Subscribed and sworn before me on 21 October 2022 in Quezon City by the affiants with
exhibit of their respective competent evidence of identity (Pages 56 & 59 & 62 of this Petition).

Document   125   ATTY ROGELIO JOSE BOLIVAR
                             NOTARY PUBLIC IN QUEZON CITY
Page   25   Commission: Administrative Matter N0 Nº 294 (2021-2022)
                             IBP OR Nº 132134 MD 2021 & PNP-OR Nº 229876 MD 2022
Book   VI   PTR OR Nº 2461/2190 / 2022-01-03 / Roll Nº 108 22 / TIN 126-07/-304
                             IBOLE Nº 95-0529789 /2021A 11 083 Quezon City
Series   2022   Address: 25/F Ransom Street - Cubao - Quezon City

Signed on 28 October 2022 in Quezon City

Respectfully

KATES JASTIN E. AGUILAR
COLLABORATING COUNSEL FOR THE PETITIONERS
Postal Address @ base of Eliseo Rio Jr
Lot 7 Block 11 Soldiers Hill
Barangay Putatan 1772 Muntinlupa City
Roll of Attorneys № 80208
IBP № 216409 – May 24, 2022
Occidental Mindoro Chapter
PTR № 3312294 – 07/15/2022
MCLE / Admitted to the Bar: May 18, 2022
0939-849-2254
katesjastin@gmail.com

eliseoriojr27@gmail.com
0917-832-9276

gusiagman2019@gmail.com
0917-817-8477

ffysaac@gmail.com
0918-925-5472

🔒 **z-p3-cdn.fbsbx.com** Done

19 Misamis Oriental Association of Coco Traders versus Department of Finance Secretary (GR № 108524) (10 November 1994) // Commissioner of Internal Revenue versus Fortune Tobacco (GR № 119761) (29 August 1996)

20 Administrative Code Book VII (Administrative Procedure) Chapter 2 (Rules and Regulations) Section 9 subsections (1) & (3)

21 Constitution Article III (Bill of Rights) Section 7

22 Constitution Article II (State Policies) Section 28

23 Constitution Article IX-C-(COMELEC) Section 2 subsection 9

ISSUES
(PURELY LEGAL ISSUES) / (QUESTIONS OF LAW)

May the Honorable Supreme Court order the respondents to preserve the subscriber / cyber traffic data log integrity / call record details corresponding to national election results transmitted from 7PM to at least 9PM of 09 May 2022?

May the Honorable Supreme Court restrain the respondents from modifying / erasing / deleting the subscriber / cyber traffic data log integrity / call record details corresponding to national election results transmitted from 7PM to at least 9PM of 09 May 2022?

May the respondents delay resolution of this case until after the 9th of November 2022 when the respondents may argue about being no longer under the duty to preserve said data in accordance with National Telecommunications Commission Memorandum Circular № 2007-04-06 in relation to the Cybercrime Prevention Law (specifically Republic Act № 10175 Section 13)?

May the respondents invoke the Data Privacy Act as excuse notwithstanding the logic that this Petition is just praying for preservation of historically-important data = not release of said historically-important data to the petitioners?

PRAYER

WHEREFORE, PREMISES CONSIDERED, it is most respectfully prayed of the Honorable Supreme Court:

1. A Temporary Restraining Order (TRO) be issued immediately enjoining the respondents to cease and desist from any act that may modify / erase / delete any part or whole of the historically important subscriber / cyber traffic data log integrity / call record details corresponding to national election results transmitted from 7PM to at least 9PM of 09 May 2022;

2. After due hearing before 9 November 2022, and/or on the basis of judicial notice of history, an ancillary writ of preliminary mandatory injunction be issued, directing the private respondent telecommunication companies (telcos) to deliver faithful copies of their respective records/details of the said historically-important data directly and exclusively to the Honorable Supreme Court; and

3. After due hearing, a final writ of mandamus be issued directing the respondents to preserve for posterity the said historically-important data.

Other reliefs just and equitable are also prayed for.

agency receives an opposition to a rule-making proposal. [18]

---

[17]   People versus William Ernest Jolliffe (GR № L-9553) 13 May 1959 () // Victorias Milling Company versus Social Security System (GR № L-16704) 17 March 1962 (114 Philippine Reports 555) // Philippine Blooming Mills versus Social Security System (GR № L-21223) 31 August 1966 (124 Philippine Reports 499)
[18]   Administrative Code Book VII (Administrative Procedure) Chapter 2 (Rules and Regulations) Section 9 subsections (1) & (3)

57.   Jurisprudence is replete with examples of legislative rules that are in the nature of subordinate legislation for implementing primary legislation by providing the details thereof. Adoption of a legislative rule generally requires hearing in the same way that laws must have the benefit of public hearing. [19] The same jurisprudence elaborates on three questions which the Court may ask when investigating delegation of legislative rule-making authority to an administrative agency. First: is the rule within the authority? Second: is it reasonable? Third: was it issued pursuant to proper procedure?

Republic Act № 8436 § 31	Republic Act № 9369 § 30
The Commission shall promulgate rules and regulations for the implementation and enforcement of this Act including such measures that will address possible difficulties and confusions ...	The Commission shall promulgate rules and regulation for the implementation and enforcement of this Act.

58.   The said "rules and regulations" in election automation legislations are **quasi-legislative** that require public hearing. Those rules are not merely "interpretative". There is no excuse for escaping from **public consultation**. Observance of mandatory due process by public consultation procedure under the Administrative Code [20] can at least lay the groundwork for minimizing the damage to democracy.

GRAVE AND IRREPARABLE INJURY TO
FREEDOM OF INFORMATION

59.   The Constitution {recognizes the people's right to information on matters of public concern} and {affords citizens access to official records & documents pertaining to official acts & transactions & decisions & research data that government may use as basis for policy development}. [21] Moreover, the Constitution {adopts and implements a policy of full public disclosure of all its transactions involving public interest} [22] and commands Comelec to {submit a comprehensive report after each election}. [23]

60.   Grave and irreparable injuries, like the sword hanging above the head Damocles, are sure to fall and behead historical truth unless a temporary restraining order (TRO) and/or preliminary mandatory injunction shall come to the rescue. The People, not the petitioners, are the ultimate beneficiaries if the Honorable Supreme Court grants the prayers in this Petition.

---

[19]   Misamis Oriental Association of Coco Traders versus Department of Finance Secretary (GR № 108524) (10 November 1994) // Commissioner of Internal Revenue versus Fortune Tobacco (GR № 119761) (29 August 1996)
[20]   Administrative Code Book VII (Administrative Procedure) Chapter 2 (Rules and Regulations) Section 9 subsections (1) & (3)
[21]   Constitution Article III (Bill of Rights) Section 7
[22]   Constitution Article II (State Policies) Section 28
[23]   Constitution Article IX-C-(COMELEC) Section 2 subsection 9

- Donate polling laptops to the school after elections.

- Save the transportation cost that returning laptops incur.

- Minimal training.

- Accurate.

POSSIBLE SOLUTIONS AFTER COURT INTERVENTION

47.   This Petition is unique, not only in the sense of being politically neutral, but more so in the sense that it aims to expose twin root causes explaining why many individuals and groups habitually rush to the Honorable Supreme Court with a glimmer of hope that judicial action may prevent or at least deter the administrative acts or omissions of respondent Comelec which is known and notorious for having a history of railroading, without public consultation, promulgation of GENERAL INSTRUCTIONS (GI) which are broad "rules" with "devils in the details" that violate Laws or Republic Acts that underwent extensive public consultations. Often, the midnight implementing rules written by shady bureaucrats, hiding under obscure technological jargon, contravene Republic Acts.

48.   The twin root causes are: first, **omission** of its duty under the laws to promulgate implementing rules after public consultation; and second, **act** of promulgating surprise midnight piecemeal general instructions without prior public consultation.

49.   The Judicial Notice Rule [16] enumerates the items which courts, including the Honorable Supreme Court, may consider for arriving at a conclusion. The "political constitution and history of the Philippines" are among the items in said enumeration. Substantially all allegations herein are within the scope of Philippine history.

50.   Petitioners respectfully wish to emphasize that the core issue in this Petition involves pure question of law and does not raise factual issues that may dump a burden of ascertaining cumbersome facts on the desk of the Honorable Supreme Court.

51.   Understandably, the Honorable Supreme Court must be free from the cumbersome burden of excavating archeological mounds of allegations to dig and ferret out truth from a seemingly insurmountable debris of fake news.

52.   Many electoral reform advocates have been calling attention to the express provision in Republic Act № 8436 Section 6, as amended by Republic Act № 9369 Section 6, under which the Comelec is authorized (not required) to use an automated election system or systems in some localities or nationwide.

---

[16]   Rules of Court Rule 129 Section 1

🔒 **z-p3-cdn.fbsbx.com**   Done

36. Good point: almost instantaneous results.

37. Bad points: Unobservable vote-counting is inherently insane. None of the voters can witness the counting of votes. Voters cannot detect vote manipulation. The system killed the protest process.

PETITION TO COMPEL COMELEC SMARTMATIC TO PRESERVE SUBSCRIBER & CYBER TRAFFIC DATA INTEGRITY (RESTRAIN ERASURE) OF NATIONAL ELECTION RESULTS TRANSMITTED FROM 7PM TO AT LEAST 9PM OF 09 MAY 2022

Page 15 of 100

38. Why spend ten billion pesos to automate precinct activities requiring only 5 to 12 hours (24 hours in extreme cases)?

39. Better approach: automate the canvass (not precinct) activities at a cost of around 300 million pesos only and yet save around 30 days.

40. Why did most first world democracies junk the Smartmatic style of automation and shift to hybrid election system?

41. Germany forbids "push button voting" that is not transparent or that requires blind faith because the voter cannot see the counting. Voting on blind faith is unconstitutional according to the Supreme Court of Germany.

42. German Slogan: "Secret Voting. Public Counting."

43. Ireland paid around 40 million Euros for voting machines from the "Nedap" Dutch company to pilot test 3 constituencies in the 2002 Irish general election and a referendum on the Treaty of Nice. Public dissatisfaction led to a decision on 23 April 2009 to scrap electronic voting system.

44. 20 years of e-voting in Netherlands fell apart in 2008. Voters prefer pen and paper.

45. Growing number of states in the USA (around 20 to 30 states) are reverting to the manual system.

46. The Hybrid System is a better alternative.

- Open-source software.

- No need for time-consuming (months-long) software review.

- No need to generate VCM hash codes in every precinct.

- No need for VCM Final Testing and Sealing (FTS).

- Donate polling laptops to the school after elections.

- Save the transportation cost that returning laptops incur.

- Minimal training.

- Accurate.

view of the unraveling of alarming events of late. [15]

[11] Former Vice President Teofisto Tayko Guingona and Rodolfo Imperial Lozada *et al* versus Comelec (GR № 191846) (06 May 2010)
[12] Constitution Article VIII Section 5 (1)
[13] Wigberto Tañada *et al* versus Edgardo Angara *et al* (GR № 118295) 02 May 1997
[14] Francisco Ibrado Chavez versus Presidential Commission on Good Government (GR № 130716) 09 December 1998
[15] Teofisto Guingona *et al* versus Comelec (GR № 191846) 06 May 2010

PETITION TO COMPEL COMELEC SMARTMATIC TO PRESERVE SUBSCRIBER & CYBER TRAFFIC DATA INTEGRITY (RESTRAIN ERASURE) OF NATIONAL ELECTION RESULTS TRANSMITTED FROM 7PM TO AT LEAST 9PM OF 09 MAY 2022

ADVOCACIES OF PETITIONER "GUS" LAGMAN

29. Here is a description of postwar Philippine elections using purely manual election system starting in year 1946. Voters first fill up their ballots by hand then (2nd) cast the ballots themselves then (3rd) insert the ballots into the ballot box.

30. After the voting period: BEI (Board of Election Inspectors) tabulate the votes manually and then physically transport the results known as ER (Election Return) to the C/MBOC (City/Municipality Board of Canvassers). The C/MBOC tabulate the ERs manually and then physically transport the results (COC) (Certificate of Canvass) to the PBOC (Provincial BOC). The PBOC tabulate the COCs manually and then physically transport the results (Provincial COC) to the Congress and then Presidential Election Tribunal for final tabulation of the party-list then senatorial then vice-presidential then presidential votes.

31. Good point: The ladder hierarchy is transparent and allows voters to witness and fully-understand the system.

32. Bad point: The process was slow. Precinct activities consume a day. Physical transport from precincts to canvassing points, and, later, the three-level canvassing steps, require four to six weeks.

33. Republic Act № 9369 authorizes the COMELEC to automate transparent, credible, fair, and accurate elections.

34. Description: Election Day: Voters shade ballot ovals corresponding to their candidate choices and then feed the ballots into a black box known as VOTE COUNTING MACHINES (VCM) that tabulate votes and printout results (ERs) which poll workers distribute according to law. VCMs electronically-transmit results to the three-level canvassing points.

35. COMELEC did not automate as such until after the 2007 elections.

36. Good point: almost instantaneous results.

37. Bad points: Unobservable vote-counting is inherently insane. None of the voters can witness the counting of votes. Voters cannot detect vote manipulation. The system killed the protest process.

which they can declare that the precious top secret, involving vital national interest, emptied into a "Recycle Bin" or "Trash" that is deeper than any cyber burial grave, gone forever, zapped.

     Proverbs 26:11

NATURE OF THE PETITION

16. This is a special civil action for mandamus aiming to compel respondents to perform an easy task requiring virtually zero budget: save transcendentally important historical data or at least share copies thereof with the Honorable Supreme Court. A simple email (containing the subject data) from any or all respondents to the Honorable Supreme Court can accomplish the task.

17. Petitioners have no more plain / speedy / adequate remedy in the ordinary course of law because the 9th of November 2022 is just a few ticks away and fast approaching.

18. Ordinary remedy is not plain because respondents refuse to budge even a single inch to a plain-and-simple request.

19. Ordinary remedy is not speedy because time flew for the past five months and respondents are still stonewalling despite exhaustive efforts by petitioners and many other patriotic citizens.

20. Ordinary remedy is not adequate because the triumvirates of Comelec and Smartmatic viz-a-viz telecommunication companies are so titanic in stature that they have not shown any interest in glancing down to spend even a few seconds of their precious time for paying some attention to tiny but patriotic individual citizens.

TIMELINESS AND RIPENESS

21. The issue is timely and ripe, perhaps even over-ripe, because the respondent telecommunication companies will soon have an excuse to delete forever the historically important data after expiration of the period of six months that has been ticking away, without missing a single heartbeat, since the 9 May 2022 elections, toward irreversible erasure this coming 9 November 2022, as the respondent telecommunication companies are, by then, no longer under any obligation to save the sensitive public document, unless and until the Honorable Supreme Court intervenes for salvation of the said nationally-important data.

22. Jurisprudence is replete with examples that spare mandamus from excessive inflexibilities of deadline rules (such as limitation statutes) in the interest of substantial justice. [10]

---

[10]   Guillerma Flordelis *et al* versus Fermin Mar *et al* (GR № L-54887) (22 May 1982) citing Volume 52 American Jurisprudence 2nd edition Page 705 and Volume 55 American Law Reports Pages 1144 to 1147

Date	Time			%			Total	
2022-05-09	8:47PM		67%	3,696,394	19%	16%	29,446,102	100%
2022-05-09	9:02PM		63%	6,037,896	19%	17%	31,175,247	100%
2022-05-09	8:02PM		63%	6,286,504	19%	17%	32,591,120	100%
2022-05-09	9:17PM		63%	6,506,755	19%	17%	33,776,639	100%
2022-05-09	9:32PM		63%	6,708,382	19%	17%	34,864,122	100%
2022-05-09	9:47PM		63%	6,896,078	19%	17%	35,841,653	100%
2022-05-09	10:02PM		64%	7,051,753	19%	17%	36,707,067	100%
2022-05-09	10:17PM		64%	7,211,145	19%	17%	37,552,903	100%
2022-05-09	10:32PM		64%	7,356,975	19%	17%	38,353,939	100%
2022-05-09	10:47PM		64%	7,497,586	19%	17%	39,136,378	100%
2022-05-09	11:02PM		64%	7,630,661	19%	17%	39,852,796	100%
2022-05-10	5:32AM		64%	8,973,187	19%	17%	47,526,696	100%
2022-05-13	3:18PM		65%	9,232,883	19%	17%	48,978,015	100%

PARTIES

10.   Petitioners are taxpayers from diverse backgrounds sharing a common desire to save Philippine democracy from the curse of the Biblical adage about an animal "swallowing its own vomit" [9] for the seventh time (1st in 2008 | 2nd in 2010 | 3rd in 2013 | 4th in 2016 | 5th in 2019 | 6th in 2022 | and probably a 7th in 2025).

11.   Respondent COMMISSION ON ELECTIONS (COMELEC) may receive copies of notices and orders at the 8th Floor of Palacio del Gobernador ‹ Andres Soriano Avenue corner General Luna Street ‹ Intramuros 1002 Manila ‹ Philippines.

12.   Petitioners anticipate the entry of appearance of the OFFICE OF THE SOLICITOR GENERAL (OSG). Petitioners undertake to furnish electronic and paper copies of this petition to the OSG as soon as possible after receiving a docket number for this petition from the Honorable Supreme Court.

13.   Respondent Smartmatic TOTAL INFORMATION MANAGEMENT (TIM) [hereafter "Smartmatic" for brevity] may receive copies of this initiatory pleading at the postal and/or email address written in its website. Petitioners are willing and ready to furnish electronic copies of this petition to Smartmatic as a "corporation" under Rule 65 Section 3 unless and until the Honorable Supreme Court orders otherwise.

14.   Respondent telecommunication companies are nominal respondents in the sense that they are bound by confidentiality obligations and/or NON-DISCLOSURE AGREEMENTS (NDA) and/or similar restrictions on liberties and/or impositions by Comelec and/or Smartmatic.

15.   Annexes "N" & "O" & "P" prove that petitioners have been, and continue to be, exerting exhaustive efforts at securing the cooperation of the respondent telecommunication companies, but their lips remain tight, unwilling to crack an opening, not even to inhale, not even to exhale, holding their breaths for the longest time, probably all the way until the 9th of November 2022, after which they can declare that the precious top secret, involving vital national interest, emptied into a "Recycle Bin" or "Trash" that is deeper than any cyber burial grave, gone forever, zapped.

counted and shown the public on 8:02pm and the uncanny constant vote ratio for all candidates for President and Vice President, Chairman George Garcia categorically said that the 20M+ figure came from PARISH PASTORAL COUNCIL FOR RESPONSIBLE VOTING (PPCRV) and not from COMELEC!"

PETITION TO COMPEL COMELEC SMARTMATIC TO PRESERVE SUBSCRIBER & CYBER TRAFFIC DATA INTEGRITY (RESTRAIN ERASURE) OF NATIONAL ELECTION RESULTS TRANSMITTED FROM 7PM TO AT LEAST 9PM OF 09 MAY 2022

"Another question that remained unanswered was could COMELEC assure the voting public that the ballots that were randomly selected, and transported to Diamond Hotel for the RANDOM MANUAL AUDIT (RMA), were never tampered in transit, considering that the watchdogs for this activity, NATIONAL MOVEMENT FOR FREE ELECTIONS (NAMFREL) and LEGAL NETWORK FOR TRUTHFUL ELECTIONS (LENTE), never observed the proper sealing of the ballot boxes, and should be the only ones who could unseal these upon arrival in the hotel."

"Unless COMELEC actually shows the transmission logs, collaborated by the telcos CALL DETAIL RECORDS (CDR), from 7pm to 8pm of May 9, then the election may most likely had been rigged."

"... uncanny constant vote ratio ..."

Presidential Candidates

DATE	TIME	votes	%	votes	%	votes	%	votes	%	votes	%	5 candidates total votes	%
2022-05-09	8:02PM	[illegible]		[illegible]		517,651		974,160		[illegible]		22,051,031	100%
2022-05-09	8:17PM	[illegible]		[illegible]		1,259,710		1,063,056		[illegible]		25,454,622	100%
2022-05-09	8:32PM	[illegible]		[illegible]		1,490,502		1,188,770		[illegible]		29,096,429	100%
2022-05-09	8:47PM	[illegible]		[illegible]		1,489,535		1,148,386		[illegible]		31,466,808	100%
2022-05-09	9:02PM	[illegible]		[illegible]		1,388,298		1,207,008		[illegible]		33,318,521	100%
2022-05-09	9:02PM	[illegible]		[illegible]		1,516,446		1,208,744		[illegible]		34,215,212	100%
2022-05-09	9:17PM	[illegible]		[illegible]		1,374,228		1,418,560		979,210		36,080,534	100%
2022-05-09	9:32PM	[illegible]		[illegible]		1,398,374		1,453,538		[illegible]		37,059,233	100%
2022-05-09	9:47PM	[illegible]		[illegible]		1,192,579		1,463,030		710,871		38,280,810	100%
2022-05-09	10:02PM	[illegible]		[illegible]		2,212,008		1,517,344		[illegible]		39,704,447	100%
2022-05-09	10:17PM	[illegible]		[illegible]		2,336,860		1,538,574		741,989		40,106,140	100%
2022-05-09	10:32PM	[illegible]		[illegible]		1,497,574		1,561,179		744,617		40,980,010	100%
2022-05-09	10:47PM	[illegible]		[illegible]		2,384,968		1,580,319		[illegible]		41,802,681	100%
2022-05-09	11:02PM	[illegible]		[illegible]		2,444,860		1,607,887		[illegible]		42,571,354	100%
2022-05-10	5:32AM	[illegible]		[illegible]		2,453,596		1,594,169		[illegible]		50,776,540	100%
2022-05-13	3:18PM	[illegible]		[illegible]		3,628,958		1,700,810		[illegible]		52,336,277	100%

Vice Presidential Candidates

DATE	TIME	Sara votes	%	Kiko votes	%	votes	%	3 candidates total votes	%
2022-05-09	8:02PM	[illegible]	63%	3,865,672	20%	[illegible]	19%	18,740,710	100%
2022-05-09	8:17PM	[illegible]	62%	4,632,451	19%	[illegible]	17%	23,803,013	100%
2022-05-09	8:32PM	[illegible]	63%	3,275,461	19%	[illegible]	15%	27,175,096	100%
2022-05-09	8:47PM	[illegible]	63%	5,696,594	19%	[illegible]	15%	29,446,182	100%
2022-05-09	9:02PM	[illegible]	63%	6,017,896	19%	[illegible]	17%	31,175,247	100%
2022-05-09	8:02PM	[illegible]	63%	6,280,504	19%	[illegible]	17%	32,591,129	100%
2022-05-09	9:17PM	[illegible]	62%	6,506,755	19%	[illegible]	17%	33,776,639	100%
2022-05-09	9:32PM	[illegible]	63%	6,208,582	19%	[illegible]	17%	34,864,172	100%
2022-05-09	9:47PM	[illegible]	63%	6,894,078	19%	[illegible]	17%	35,841,653	100%
2022-05-09	10:02PM	[illegible]	64%	7,051,753	19%	[illegible]	17%	36,707,067	100%
2022-05-09	10:17PM	[illegible]	64%	7,211,149	19%	[illegible]	17%	37,552,903	100%
2022-05-09	10:32PM	[illegible]	64%	7,356,975	19%	[illegible]	17%	38,353,939	100%
2022-05-09	10:47PM	[illegible]	64%	7,407,588	19%	[illegible]	17%	39,136,378	100%
2022-05-09	11:02PM	[illegible]	64%	7,630,661	19%	[illegible]	17%	39,852,796	100%
2022-05-10	5:32AM	[illegible]	64%	8,973,187	19%	[illegible]	16%	47,526,696	100%
2022-05-13	3:18PM	[illegible]	64%	9,232,883	19%	[illegible]	17%	48,978,015	100%

that this required printing process takes at least 30 minutes, sometimes up to more than an hour. Thus, in the case of the 2022 election, the earliest transmissions would have been made at around 7:30pm."

"So, using the same graph that COMELEC presented in the Forum, and enlarging it to focus on the few hours after transmission started at 7:30pm (Pic4), it will be clearly seen that the data shown to the public by the Transparency Server are **highly irregular**!"

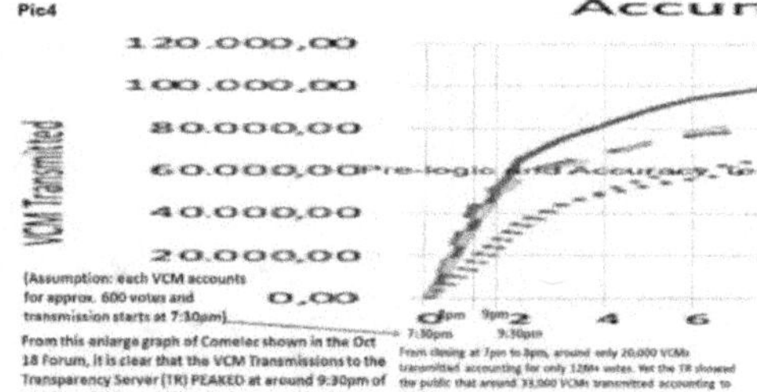

From this enlarge graph of Comelec shown in the Oct 18 Forum, it is clear that the VCM Transmissions to the Transparency Server (TR) PEAKED at around 9:30pm of May 9, and NOT at 8:02pm as shown to the public.

From closing at 7pm to 8pm, around only 20,000 VCMs transmitted accounting for only 12M+ votes. Yet the TR showed the public that around 33,000 VCMs transmitted accounting to the PEAK 20M+ votes counted in that same first hour.

"It is clearly shown that transmission peaked around 2 hours after VCMs started transmission, at around 9:30pm, **not** 8:02pm. The graph also shows that at 8:02pm, around 20,000 VCMs transmitted their data which will account for only 12M votes, **not a PEAK** 20M+ votes, assuming that each VCM handles 600 voters."

"The fact that COMELEC was able to show the graph in the October 18 Forum, means that it has the compilation of transmission logs from 7pm to 9pm, which we have been asking since July 15, 2022. Why they did not show this to the public during the Forum, and instead showed a graph that would tend to show that nothing irregular happened, is questionable. **But looking closer at that graph they presented** showed that COMELEC is likely hiding something in its assessment of the last election. In fact, when questioned about the PEAK 20M+ votes that was counted and shown the public on 8:02pm and the uncanny constant vote ratio for all candidates for President and Vice President, Chairman George Garcia categorically said that the 20M+ figure came from PARISH PASTORAL COUNCIL FOR RESPONSIBLE VOTING (PPCRV) and not from COMELEC!"

PETITION TO COMPEL COMELEC SMARTMATIC TO PRESERVE SUBSCRIBER &
CYBER TRAFFIC DATA INTEGRITY (RESTRAIN ERASURE) OF NATIONAL ELECTION
RESULTS TRANSMITTED FROM 7PM TO AT LEAST 9PM OF 09 MAY 2022

Page 8 of 100

"Instead of showing transmission logs to account for the questionable PEAK of 20M+ shown to the public in the Transparency Server, COMELEC instead showed a graph (Pic3) where it explained that there are no irregularities in the transmission of data in the May 9 election because it conforms to the transmissions of past AES elections 2010, 2013, 2016, and 2019, except that in the 2022 election, more VCMs were used."

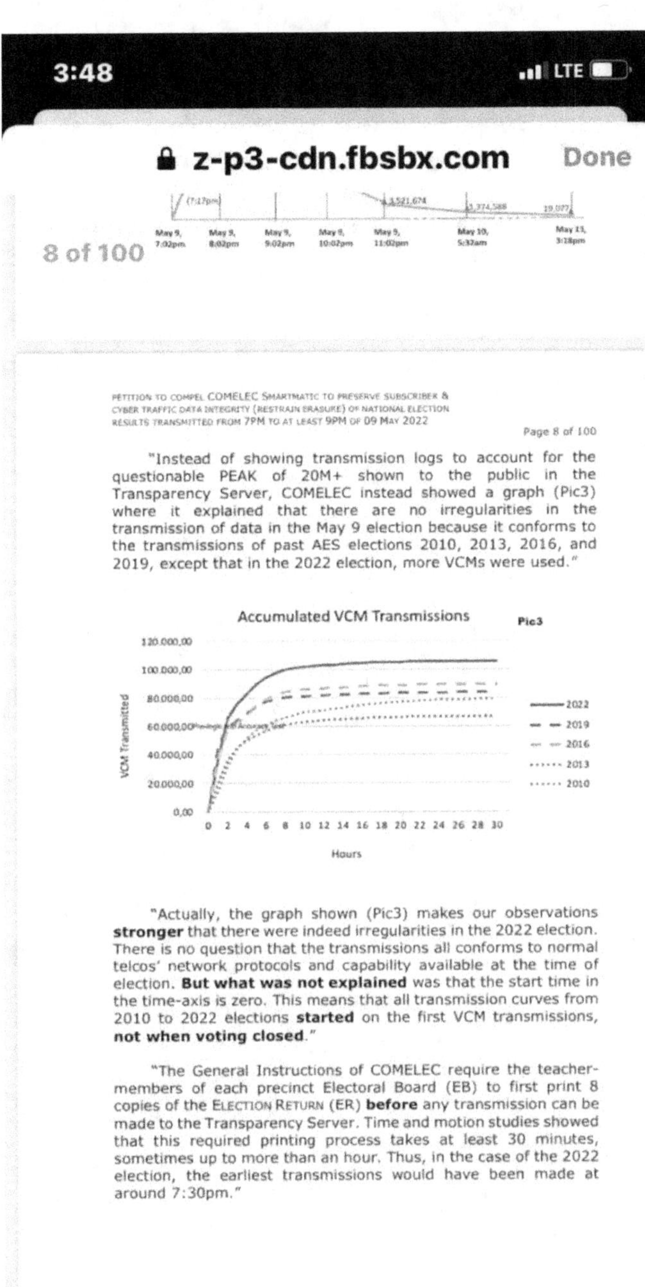

"Actually, the graph shown (Pic3) makes our observations **stronger** that there were indeed irregularities in the 2022 election. There is no question that the transmissions all conforms to normal telcos' network protocols and capability available at the time of election. **But what was not explained** was that the start time in the time-axis is zero. This means that all transmission curves from 2010 to 2022 elections **started** on the first VCM transmissions, **not when voting closed.**"

"The General Instructions of COMELEC require the teacher-members of each precinct Electoral Board (EB) to first print 8 copies of the ELECTION RETURN (ER) **before** any transmission can be made to the Transparency Server. Time and motion studies showed that this required printing process takes at least 30 minutes, sometimes up to more than an hour. Thus, in the case of the 2022 election, the earliest transmissions would have been made at around 7:30pm."

from 7:02pm to 8:02pm of May 9, 2022, to account for the incredible 20M+ votes counted just one hour after the voting [...]. This is to dispel any and all doubts about grossly [...]usible results shown in the Transparency Server and restore [...]eople's trust in the 2022 elections."

LATEST VIRAL SOCIAL MEDIA POSTINGS
<https://www.facebook.com/eliseoriojr>

"On October 18, 2022, the Ateneo School of Government, thru a non-partisan, pro-democracy, Participate PH, organized a Forum on 'The COMELEC Assessment of the 2022 National and Local Elections'. Guest Speaker was COMELEC Chairperson George Garcia. We attended the Forum hoping that the irregularities we have observed during the May 9 election will be resolved. Last July 15, we have written COMELEC regarding our observation that COMELEC has to prove by showing actual transmission logs that indeed a PEAK 20M+ votes were counted at the first hour of counting from 7pm to 8pm, and only 13.2M+ votes were counted in the second hour from 8pm to 9pm on May 9. Such results (shown in Pic1 and Pic2) are mathematically, logically and statistically **highly improbable** if not **impossible**."

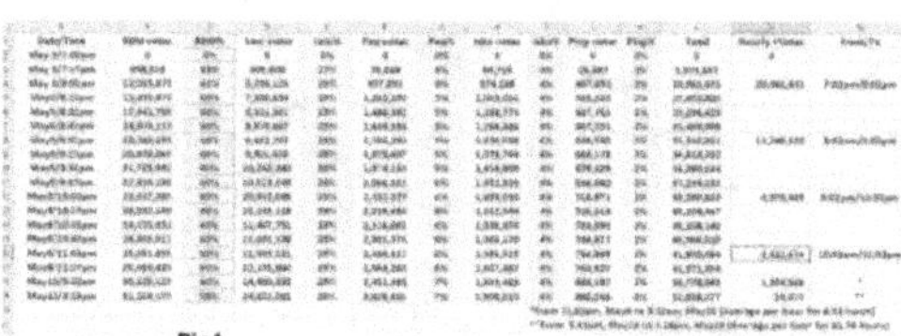

Pic1

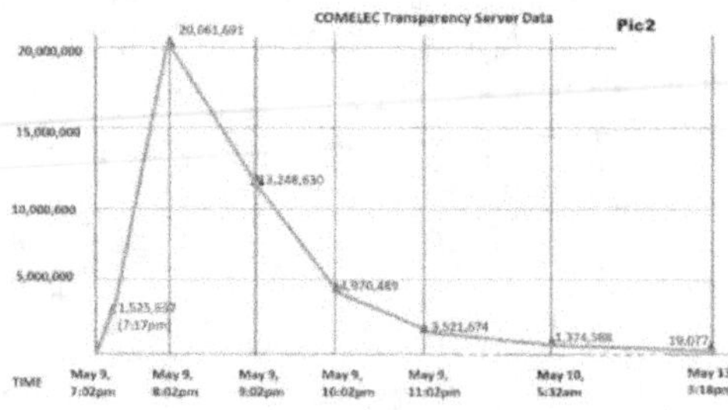

🔒 **z-p3-cdn.fbsbx.com**   Done

"This is the **first** time in our election history, and maybe in the history of the whole world, that the number of votes counted **peaked** at the very **first hour** in a four-day counting period."

PETITION TO COMPEL COMELEC SMARTMATIC TO PRESERVE SUBSCRIBER & CYBER TRAFFIC DATA INTEGRITY (RESTRAIN ERASURE) OF NATIONAL ELECTION RESULTS TRANSMITTED FROM 7PM TO AT LEAST 9PM OF 09 MAY 2022

Page 6 of 100

"It would have been easy for Comelec to have answered our letter by simply showing that indeed more than 20M votes were counted in the first hour because these large number of votes were the basis of their explanation to the public that the highly statistically improbable constant vote ratios of ALL candidates for president and vice president, that appeared in every update of the counting from the very beginning to end, is possible using the 'law of large numbers' theory."

"Instead, they redirected us to get our answers from the JOINT CONGRESSIONAL OVERSIGHT COMMITTEE ON AUTOMATED ELECTION SYSTEM (JCOC-AES) and the COMELEC ADVISORY COUNCIL (CAC), when the data we are asking for are supposed to have originated from Comelec. If Comelec cannot show the public that at least 2,000 transmission reports were received electronically that have the date/time stamp between 7pm and 7:17pm of May 9, 2022 then the only conclusion that can be derived is that such numbers were **pre-loaded** into the transparency and/or the Comelec servers."

"We challenge Comelec to demonstrate to the public that all activities required in its General Instructions, including the printing of the ER, can be done in less than 17 minutes before any transmission is made. And for that matter, show the public, in a time and motion demo, the actual time it takes for the Election Board, from closing the voting, printing of ERs, to the transmission of the ERs. We challenge Comelec to show the public at least 2,000 Transmission Reports that have date/time stamps between 7:00pm and 7:17pm to account for the 1,525,637 votes shown in the Transparency Server at 7:17pm. We further appeal to the poll watchdog PARISH PASTORAL COUNCIL FOR RESPONSIBLE VOTING (PPCRV) to tell the public whether, in their manual count of the printed ERs given to them, they could account for at least 2,000 Transmission Reports of ERs with date/time stamps between 7pm and 7:17pm. If none of these can be shown or proven, then the data being shown in the Transparency Server is fraudulent from the very beginning."

"We appeal to the JCOC-AES to expedite the release of these data, disclose to the public the date/time stamps of all transmission reports of ERs from the VCMs via telcos to the Transparency Server from 7:02pm to 8:02pm of May 9, 2022, to account for the incredible 20M+ votes counted just one hour after the voting closed. This is to dispel any and all doubts about grossly implausible results shown in the Transparency Server and restore the people's trust in the 2022 elections."

🔒 **z-p3-cdn.fbsbx.com**   Done

---

[8] The quotations of said viral social media postings are not raising factual issue burdens to the Supreme Court. The quotations are just descriptions of the background that led to the formulation of the purely legal questions of law in the Executive Summary and Prayer of this Petition.

PETITION TO COMPEL COMELEC SMARTMATIC TO PRESERVE SUBSCRIBER & CYBER TRAFFIC DATA INTEGRITY (RESTRAIN ERASURE) OF NATIONAL ELECTION RESULTS TRANSMITTED FROM 7PM TO AT LEAST 9PM OF 09 MAY 2022

"It would take at least 30 minutes, after the last voter casted his/her vote after closing time, to officially close the voting, set up the VCM for printing, print 8 copies of the ER (with unavoidable printing break time delays necessary for replenishing rolls of depleted thermal printer paper), affixing the signatures of the teachers on each and every ER set or a total of 8 ER sets, and then give some time for the poll watchers to scrutinize the printed ER. Then and only then can the ER be transmitted electronically to the Transparency Server."

"The earliest transmissions then would occur **after** 7:30pm. It is therefore **impossible** for the Transparency Server to have shown to the public 1.5M votes by 7:17pm!"

"Even if assuming that indeed all requirements of the Comelec General Instructions were complied with within 17 minutes, and transmissions began, as shown by the first result of the Transparency Server at 7:17pm, that would mean that the 20,061,691 votes shown to the public at 8:02pm were the result of transmissions from the VCMs to the Transparency Server in just 45 minutes."

"No transmissions were made in the first 15 minutes after voting closed because of the requirements of the General Instructions, which include printing of 8 copies of the ER, which must first be done before the ER could be transmitted. That would now set the rate of transmissions received by the Transparency Server and we could then compute that the rate of votes counted in 60 minutes or in 1 hour would be 26,748,921 votes per hour."

"Yet in the second hour of counting, from 8:02pm to 9:02pm, only 13,248,630 votes were counted, less than half the rate of counting established in the first hour."

"This is very illogical because much more VCMs should have been ready to transmit than the first hour, during which precinct officials were still preparing the ERs for transmission. Considering that numerous voters who were in the vicinity of the precincts at the 7pm closing time were still allowed to vote, therefore, almost all would have voted by the second hour."

"This is the **first** time in our election history, and maybe in the history of the whole world, that the number of votes counted **peaked** at the very **first hour** in a four-day counting period."

2022 | 10 | 18 | Judicial Affidavit of Eliseo Mijares Rio Jr   5

 Joint Congressional Oversight Committee (JCOC)
 Pastoral Council for Responsible Voting (PPCRV)

PETITION TO COMPEL COMELEC SMARTMATIC TO PRESERVE SUBSCRIBER &
CYBER TRAFFIC DATA INTEGRITY (RESTRAIN ERASURE) OF NATIONAL ELECTION
RESULTS TRANSMITTED FROM 7PM TO AT LEAST 9PM OF 09 MAY 2022

Page 4 of 100

SUMMARY OF VIRAL SOCIAL MEDIA POSTINGS [8]
<https://www.facebook.com/eliseoriojr>

"At 7:17pm of May 9, 2022, just seventeen (17) minutes after voting closed at 7pm, the Comelec Transparency Server showed the public its first counting result of 1,525,637 votes. These number of votes would come from at least 2,000 clustered precincts VOTE COUNTING MACHINES (VCM)."

"The Comelec General Instructions to the teacher members of the Election Board require, among others, that eight (8) printed and signed copies of the precinct ELECTION RETURN (ER) must first be done before any transmission can be made. The printing alone took the longest time for the thermal printer in the VCM is slow."

"Comelec itself admitted on record = judicial admission before the Supreme Court during the hearing of oral arguments resulting to the promulgation of the 8 March 2016 landmark Supreme Court decision in {Bagumbayan Volunteers for a New Philippines and [Senator] Richard Juico Gordon *et al* versus Comelec and Smartmatic *et al*} (GR № 222731) = that it takes **at least thirteen (13) seconds** to print each *"resibo"* or VOTER VERIFIABLE PAPER AUDIT TRAIL (VVPAT) which will result in adding at least two (2) hours to the voting process."

"This is the same printer used to print the eight (8) copies of the Election Returns (ER). The printed VVPAT contains only the names of one (1) President, one (1) Vice President, twelve (12) Senators, one (1) Party List Representative, and around an equal number of names for local government positions {Congress Rep, Governor, Vice Governor, *Bokal*, Mayor, Vice Mayor, *Konsehal*}."

"The printed ER is much longer, containing the names of ten (10) presidential candidates, nine (9) vice presidential candidates, sixty-four (64) senatorial candidates, one hundred seventy-seven (177) party list candidates, and around an equal number of candidates for local positions."

[8]   The quotations of said viral social media postings are not raising factual issue burdens to the Supreme Court. The quotations are just descriptions of the background that led to the formulation of the purely legal questions of law in the Executive Summary and Prayer of this Petition.

5   JCOC AES 28 August 2014 deliberations TSN Page 90 quoting COMELEC Chairman Sixto Serrano Brillantes

PETITION TO COMPEL COMELEC SMARTMATIC TO PRESERVE SUBSCRIBER & CYBER TRAFFIC DATA INTEGRITY (RESTRAIN ERASURE) OF NATIONAL ELECTION RESULTS TRANSMITTED FROM 7PM TO AT LEAST 9PM OF 09 MAY 2022

Page 3 of 100

8.   The period of six months (from the May 9, 2022 elections) is soon to expire within a few days from today = on the 9th of November 2022. Time is of the essence.

9.   This Urgent Petition does not violate the Data Privacy Act because this Petition is just praying for data preservation = not for releasing sensitive data to the petitioners.

EXHAUSTION OF ADMINISTRATIVE REMEDIES

DOCUMENT DATE			LETTERS/PLEADINGS	ANNEX IN THIS PETITION
			Procedures rendering improbable (almost impossible) transmission of election result within an hour from closing of polls	A & B Pages 22 to 33
2022	07	12	Letter requesting from COMELEC proof of transmission of data from vote counting machines to the transparency server	C & D Pages 34 to 37
2022	07	15	COMELEC En Banc Secretary Director Consuelo B Diola Transmittal Memo № 221140 to COMELEC Executive Director Bartolome J Sinocruz	E Page 38
2022	07	31	COMELEC Fire	F
2022	08	03	Letter expressing concern about the Sunday night COMELEC fire to Commissioner Marlon Casquejo	G Page 40
2022	08	15	reply of Commissioner Marlon S Casquejo	H Page 41
2022	08	23	Letter to JCOC [6]	I Pages 42 to 44
2022	08	23	Letter to Comelec Advisory Council	J Pages 45 to 47
2022	08	25	Response to Casquejo's non-responsive reply	K Page 48
2022	10	10	Letter of Ma. Asuncion Q. Hipolito, MD, to PPCRV [7]	
2022	10	10	Letter of Ma. Asuncion Q. Hipolito, MD, to Party	
2022	10	18	Letter to DITO Tele-community	N Page 51
2022	10	18	Letter to Globe Telecom	O Page 52
2022	10	18	Letter to Smart Communications	P Page 53
2022	10	18	Judicial Affidavit of Franklin Fayloga Ysaac	Q
2022	10	18	Judicial Affidavit of Augusto Cadeliña Lagman	R
2022	10	18	Judicial Affidavit of Eliseo Mijares Rio Jr	S

6   Joint Congressional Oversight Committee (JCOC)
7   Pastoral Council for Responsible Voting (PPCRV)

[3] FINANCIAL EXECUTIVES INSTITUTE OF THE PHILIPPINES (FINEX) Former President, Software App Developer for Banks, Consultancies in the Bank of Saipan and select Banks in the Philippine, Franklin Financials Consultancy

PETITION TO COMPEL COMELEC SMARTMATIC TO PRESERVE SUBSCRIBER & CYBER TRAFFIC DATA INTEGRITY (RESTRAIN ERASURE) OF NATIONAL ELECTION RESULTS TRANSMITTED FROM 7PM TO AT LEAST 9PM OF 09 MAY 2022

Page 2 of 100

EXECUTIVE SUMMARY

1.   The Election Automation Law {Republic Act № 8436 Section 27 as amended by Republic Act № 9369 Section 27 effective since 10 February 2007} requires the COMMISSION ON ELECTIONS (COMELEC) and the COMELEC ADVISORY COUNCIL (CAC) to monitor / evaluate / implement the Election Automation Law and submit a report within six months from the date of election to the JOINT CONGRESSIONAL OVERSIGHT COMMITTEE FOR AUTOMATION OF THE ELECTION SYSTEM (JCOC AES).

2.   NATIONAL TELECOMMUNICATIONS COMMISSION (NTC) Memorandum Circular № 2007-04-06 requires public telecommunication entities to retain telecommunication traffic data log and CALL DETAIL RECORDS (CDR).

3.   The Cybercrime Prevention Law (effective since 12 September 2012) (specifically Republic Act № 10175 Section 13) requires preservation of subscriber information and traffic data integrity for at least six (6) months.

4.   Previous submissions of COMELEC reports to the JCOC AES had habitually been close to the last day of the "six months" period and sometimes even beyond the last day. All previous submissions contain no report on relevant cyber traffic log / CDR data because of the clever and convenient excuse that telecommunication companies (hereafter "telco" or "telcos" for brevity) erase/delete the said data after expiration of the period of six months.

5.   Plain common sense and telcos themselves admit that they keep records of such historically important data. [4]

6.   Plain common sense and the COMELEC itself admit that it (COMELEC) has authority to keep and even "expropriate" such historically important data. [5]

7.   Why is COMELEC hiding such historically important data?

---

[4]   JCOC AES 28 August 2014 deliberations TSN Pages (21 to 23) & (28 to 30) & 84 quoting PLDT First Vice President Atty. Florentino D. Mabasa Jr.

[5]   JCOC AES 28 August 2014 deliberations TSN Page 90 quoting COMELEC Chairman Sixto Serrano Brillantes

3:41   ·ıl LTE 🔋

🔒 **z-p3-cdn.fbsbx.com**   Done

Republic of the Philippines
SUPREME COURT
Manila

En Banc

ELISEO MIJARES RIO JR. [1]
AUGUSTO CADELIÑA LAGMAN [2]
FRANKLIN FAYLOGA YSAAC [3]
   Petitioners

   versus

COMMISSION ON ELECTIONS (COMELEC)
SMARTMATIC TOTAL INFORMATION MANAGEMENT
DITO TELECOMMUNITY
GLOBE TELECOM
SMART COMMUNICATIONS
   Respondents

PETITION
FOR MANDAMUS WITH PRAYER
FOR TEMPORARY RESTRAINING ORDER
TO COMPEL PRESERVATION AND/OR
RESTRAIN ALTERATION/ERASURE/DELETION OF
SUBSCRIBER AND CYBER TRAFFIC DATA INTEGRITY
OF TELECOM TRANSMISSIONS OF NATIONAL ELECTION RESULTS
FROM 7PM TO AT LEAST 9PM OF 09 MAY 2022 PHILIPPINES TIME

Petitioners, with the assistance of volunteer lawyers, most respectfully submit this politically-neutral urgent petition, involving transcendental national interest, unto the Honorable Supreme.

---

[1] DEPARTMENT OF INFORMATION & COMMUNICATIONS TECHNOLOGY (DICT) Secretary and COMELEC Advisory Council Chairman until 1 July 2019, NATIONAL TELECOMMUNICATIONS COMMISSION Commissioner (until 2003), Ret Brigadier General since 27 October 2000, Philippine Military Academy Instructor (until 1974), Electronics & Communications Engineer 1971 Board Exam 4th Placer

[2] COMELEC Commissioner (until 2012), NATIONAL MOVEMENT FOR FREE ELECTIONS (NAMFREL) President, Manila Times "Let's Face IT" Column Writer

[3] FINANCIAL EXECUTIVES INSTITUTE OF THE PHILIPPINES (FINEX) Former President, Software App Developer for Banks, Consultancies in the Bank of Saipan and select Banks in the Philippine, Franklin Financials Consultancy

---

PETITION TO COMPEL COMELEC SMARTMATIC TO PRESERVE SUBSCRIBER & CYBER TRAFFIC DATA INTEGRITY (RESTRAIN ERASURE) OF NATIONAL ELECTION RESULTS TRANSMITTED FROM 7PM TO AT LEAST 9PM OF 09 MAY 2022

EXECUTIVE SUMMARY

1.   The Election Automation Law {Republic Act № 8436 Section 27 as amended by Republic Act № 9369 Section 27 effective since

oooooo

52
Update – Nov. 3, 2022 –
7PM – NYET –
Sad Development – PPCRV + CBCP + Comelec

A very sad development.

One of our truth warriors took the initiative of requesting from ppcrv, accredited citizens arm by comelec, and church assisted organization.

When our truth warrior attempted to get the CBCP to convince ppcrv to help us get copies of transmission reports from ppcrv as we have not been getting positive response from them, she was informed that ppcrv is an independent body which has its own life.

If that is the case, then we are asking CBCP why add parish pastoral before it's name if they don't have oversight even on governance issue.

When I asked former Namfrel Chairman and our colleague Gus Lagman what happened to a Namfrel which has lost its status as citizens arm which has performed well in the past election, he said it was Comelec who decided to accredit ppcrv and dropped Namfrel . Politics inside? Your guess is as good as mine.

Now, during the May 9 election, ppcrv echoed the results announced by Comelec and even during the Ateneo sponsored forum, the ppcrv representative confirmed what the comelec chair said it was the cleanest and most credible election as there were no election protest that ever prospered. When General Rio sent query to Comelec to explain the disparity in the transmission in transparency, the comelec chair pointed to ppcrv as the source of that report.

Nagtuturuan sila!!

Now, read this letter last October 10 by our truth warrior to ppcrv president and her response.

Nag echo chamber Silang dalawa.

Turuan na naman !!Pasahan and no accountability ! Why call itself citizens arm when ordinary citizen like our truth warrior is requesting for a piece of document which they acquire from Comelec and they have the gall to deny her that. If that's the case then it's time to remove their accreditation and to ask their volunteers to resign. In fact, we received reports when some pocrv volunteers were questioning the ERs, they were told to quiet down and they left their job as pocrv volunteers instead .

Now, when we meet with our lawyers and we are studying the possibility of including ppcrv as another respondent in the case as it has admitted it has received transmission reports during election.

As proof, we got a copy from one ppcrv volunteer who gave us one transmission report which was time stamped received at 8:02 and we published that transmission report in this fb page . We need just one transmission report from ppcrv during the first hour to prove there were transmissions made on that hour .

Why ppcrv ? Why CBCP ?

Time to find a credible citizens arm !! We need to get Namfrel back !!

October 10, 2022

MS. EVELYN SINGSON
Chairperson
Parish Pastoral Council for Responsible Voting
Pope Pius XII Catholic Center
UN Avenue, Ermita, Manila

Dear Madame Singson:

Good day and I hope this letter finds you in good heal
CONGRATULATIONS on being hailed as the new Chair of PPCRV

I am Dr. Ason Hipolito, a core member of the ***People's Movement f
Truth and Electoral Reforms (PMTER)***, initiated last May 20
after the elections.

This people's initiative was formed from a convergence of civilia
observation that a very hasty and non-transparent canvassing start
on the evening of May 09,2022, which produced an unprecedent
volume of votes in the first hour and unusual ratio/proportion of t
Presidential, Vice-Presidential and Senatorial results, and that,
many Math and IT experts are statistically improbable.

Prior to this 2022 Elections, the 2019 mid-term Elections was al
beset with such suspicious results after a 7-hour glitch eventua
welcomed none of the Opposition Candidates, even into one or t
of the lowest ranks, inspite of their wide-based coverage. Many
experts and civil opinions said that it was statistically improbable t
but we had no evidence then, and was forced to accept the pain
result.

Amidst the confusion and suspicion after the May 09, 2022 Electio
three Gentlemen, experts in their own right, surfaced in social med
and their knowledgeable posts took the words from our questioni
minds and gave us an affirmation that we are not hallucinating w
our suspicions. Their careers revolved around digital information a
technology and are trustworthy authorities in their respective fields
expertise. As none of them knew each other before the elections a
supported different candidates from different political parties, t
Truth aNd Transparency Trio (TNTrio) consider it Divi
Providence that they met and are now leading us in fighting togeth
in search of TRUTH.⬛⬛⬛⬛⬛⬛⬛⬛⬛⬛⬛⬛

MR. FRANKLIN F. YSAAC has a degree in Foreign Service and Business Administration, trained in Forex Bourse Program, Executive Development Program and Credit Seminar under CitiBank NA in Florida; taught Banking at De La Salle University, Manila and Ateneo De Manila University, Makati campus; did Consultancy work at Asian Development Bank and other various local and foreign banks, and local businesses; Career positions held: he rose up the ladder from Clerk to Manager, Vice-President and President of several banks. He was a former President of the Financial Executives Institute of the Philippines (FinEx). Presently, Mr. Ysaac is a *Software Application Provider* for Financial institutions of products dealing with treasury, forex, securities financing, accounting and other systems and the President of Franklin Financials Consultancy Phils. Inc. since 1999.

RET. BRIG. GENERAL ELISEO M. RIO, JR. is a licensed *Electronics and Communications Engineer* (4th Board Placer, 1971), held various positions and assignments, notably as Head, AFP Research and Development Center Communication-Electronics Group (1985-1988), Group Commander of Military Intelligence Group 21 and Electronics Technical Intelligence Group of the ISAFP (1988-1992), and Chief of the AFP Communications, Electronics and Information Systems Service (1999-2000). Upon retirement, he was appointed Commissioner of the National Telecommunications Commission (2001-2002); *Undersecretary for Special Concerns of the Department of Information and Communications Technology* (DICT, 2016) and held supervisory roles in agencies like the Cybercrime Investigation Coordination Center, National Privacy Commission, National Disaster Risk Reduction and Management Council and the *COMELEC Advisory Council (CAC)*. He was appointed DICT Officer In Charge (2017-2018) and *DICT Acting Secretary* on 2018-2019.

CHAIRMAN AUGUSTO C. LAGMAN is a convenor of the Movement for Good Governance, lead convenor of TransparentElections.org.ph, former President of the Information Technology Foundation of the Philippines and the Philippine Computer Society, former Chair of Vinta Systems, Inc. (*developer of artificial intelligence-oriented software products*), the *Founding Chairperson of STI* and various STI campus colleges, and a Director of STI Recto, Manila and Biometrix Technologies, Inc.

Chairman Lagman joined the *National Citizens' Movement For Free Elections (NAMFREL)* as a Volunteer in 1983 and became a Member of its National Council from 1992-2007 and 2012-2022. As head of the Systems Committee, he managed the implementation of NAMFREL's automated parallel counts (Operation Quick Count) from 1984-2007 for 10 national elections. In 1993, he was part of the team organized by COMELEC Chair Christian Monsod that *studied the various options available in automating elections*, leading to the 1996 ARMM automated elections and the enactment of the Automation Law (R.A.8436) in 1997.

Automation Law (R.A.8436) in 1997.

He was one of the eight individuals who petitioned the Supreme Court in 2003 to nullify the anomalous bidding of a P1.3Billion COMELEC contract for the acquisition of Automated Counting Machines, which the SC granted. On 2006, he was part of the Technical Working Group that helped craft the amendments to R.A.8436, resulting in the enactment of the current automation law, R.A. 9369. Chairman Lagman is the Immediate Past National Chairman of NAMFREL from 2018-2022. He also served as a *Commissioner of the COMELEC* from 2011-2012.

As Filipinos who have the Constitutional RIGHT OF SUFFRAGE: to vote and ensure that our vote is counted, we and other citizens/netizens decisively joined and support the TNTrio as the apolitical PMTER, in petitioning the COMELEC to open 750 precincts randomly selected thru a tambiolo for a manual recount of its ballots, to allow an audit of the corresponding SD Cards by independent IT experts, and to furnish the PMTER proofs of Transmission Reports (TRs) and Call Detail Reports (CDRs), especially that of the first hours of canvassing, to prove to us that there was truly an **authentic transmission of legitimate electoral results**.

With this grave violation of TRANSPARENCY against our recent electoral process, we deem it necessary to inform the whole electorate of our sovereign power over the COMELEC to demand ACCOUNTABILITY from them.

For a start, we initiated a Signature Drive to gather signatures of Filipinos of legal age, to be submitted with our Petition Letter to the COMELEC. However, after more than four months of planning and field work, we have achieved a miniscule fraction of our target of two (2) million signatures, which is largely because of a lack of awareness amongst the electorate nationwide and the fear to be red-tagged.

We have sent Letters of Request from the COMELEC to furnish us, being Filipino Citizens, copies of the TRs and CDRs, but their response was avoidant and was referring us to the Joint Congressional Oversight Committee and the COMELEC Advisory Council, who do not technically have the hard copies of the said documents.

With these circumstances, we cannot just draw back because failure to divulge this equates to INJUSTICE by subjecting the Filipino people to an **illegitimate leadership** selected by **commercially-driven entities**.

In this regard, being a non- partisan lay movement that works assiduously for Clean, Honest, Accurate, Meaningful, and Peaceful elections in the country, may we ask your help as we strengthen our evidences against the digital manipulation the TNTrio has found?

We have sent Letters of Request from the COMELEC to furnish us, being Filipino Citizens, copies of the TRs and CDRs, but their response was avoidant and was referring us to the Joint Congressional Oversight Committee and the COMELEC Advisory Council, who do not technically have the hard copies of the said documents.

With these circumstances, we cannot just draw back because failure to divulge this equates to INJUSTICE by subjecting the Filipino people to an **illegitimate leadership** selected by **commercially-driven entities**.

In this regard, being a non- partisan lay movement that works assiduously for Clean, Honest, Accurate, Meaningful, and Peaceful elections in the country, may we ask your help as we strengthen our evidences against the digital manipulation the TNTrio has found?

May we ask for photocopies of the TRANSMISSION REPORTS and ELECTORAL RECEIPTS, especially the earliest ones transmitted during the first few hours of canvassing, since these were furnished to political parties, NAMFREL and PPCRV? These would help prove that it is really impossible to transmit the 20 million votes in a span of 62 minutes (as shown on the Transparency Server at 8:02PM after closing of polls) as demonstrated by DICT Sec. Eli Rio.

I am attaching some of the social media posts and Facebook links of the TNTrio regarding this issue, to give you a glimpse of their findings.

https://youtu.be/dfbsVnCljXw

https://www.facebook.com/franklin.ysaac

https://www.facebook.com/eliseoriojr

I am fervently hoping that your organization will have a positive response on our request for our Cause, in behalf of the Filipino electorate, in the name of JUSTICE and DEMOCRACY FOR OUR COUNTRY. I will be waiting for your response and thank you for your kind attention.

Sincerely,

(sgd)_________________________
MA. ASUNCION Q. HIPOLITO, MD
PMTER Core Member
CP# 0939-3773300

2

6:10   .ıl LTE 🔋

✕   PPCRV Letter to PMTER 0...    

 PARISH PASTORAL COUNCIL
FOR RESPONSIBLE VOTING

2 November 2022

MA. ASUNCION Q. HIPOLITO, MD
Core Member
People's Movement for Truth and Electoral Reforms (PMTER)

Dear Dr. Hipolito,

This is in response to your letter dated October 10, 2022 requesting PPCRV to share photocopies of the Transmission Reports and Electoral Receipts with your organization and the TNTrio.

We understand, however, that your team, through Mr. Franklin Ysaac, Ret. Brig. Gen. Eliseo Rio, Jr., and Mr. Augusto Lagman, has also made a prior similar request with the COMELEC. In view of this, we deem it proper to wait for the official response of COMELEC before we process your request for the same data.

Nonetheless, all data that we have is available for your perusal and reproduction.

Let us know how we can be of further help.

Thank you.

Sincerely,

EVELYN R. SINGSON
Chairperson

oooooo

53
Update – Nov. 2, 2022 –
7PM – NYET
General Rio post vs Comelec Spx

Sharing from the post of our colleague General Rio after the response by Comelec Spox to our petition.

Now they have to respond to our petition before the SC. If they only gave us what we want last July 15 Hindi na Sana umabot sa SC.

Abangan na lang natin sagot nila

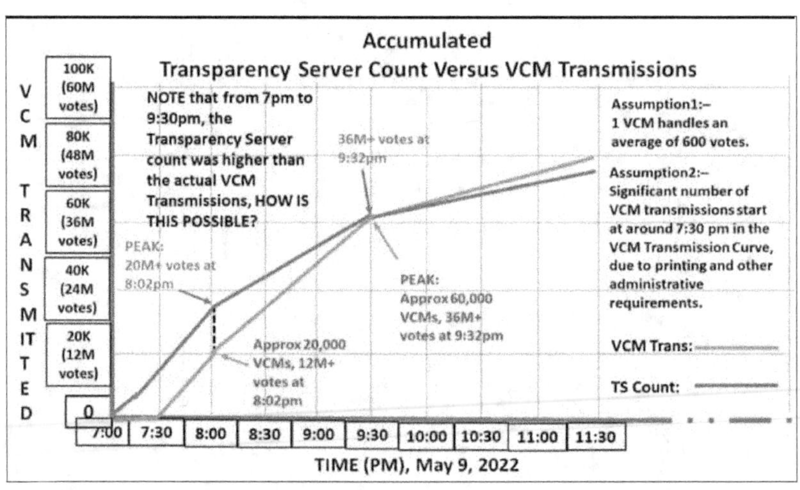

Date/Time	BBM votes	BBM%	Leni votes	Leni%	Paq votes	Paq%	Isko votes	Isko%	Ping votes	Ping%	Total	Hourly +Votes	from/To
May 9/7:02pm	0	0%	0	0%	0	0%	0	0%	0	0%	0	0	
May 9/7:17pm	958,219	63%	409,608	27%	76,668	5%	54,755	4%	26,387	2%	1,525,637		
May 9/8:02pm	12,065,875	60%	5,796,125	29%	957,851	5%	874,188	4%	407,652	2%	20,061,691	20,061,691	7:02pm/8:02pm
May9/8:17pm	15,339,878	60%	7,288,834	29%	1,262,192	5%	1,063,656	4%	505,265	2%	25,459,825		
May9/8:32pm	17,541,799	60%	8,311,501	29%	1,486,592	5%	1,188,776	4%	567,761	2%	29,096,429		
May9/8:47pm	18,975,119	60%	8,979,607	29%	1,639,535	5%	1,268,386	4%	607,251	2%	31,469,898		
May9/9:02pm	20,084,651	60%	9,492,702	28%	1,766,290	5%	1,830,088	4%	636,590	2%	33,310,321	13,248,630	8:02pm/9:02pm
May9/9:17pm	20,978,083	60%	9,921,820	28%	1,879,407	5%	1,378,744	4%	660,178	2%	34,818,232		
May9/9:32pm	21,725,982	60%	10,282,280	28%	1,974,234	5%	1,418,809	4%	679,229	2%	36,080,534		
May9/9:47pm	22,410,199	60%	10,613,144	28%	2,066,021	6%	1,453,828	4%	696,040	2%	37,239,232		
May9/10:02pm	23,017,285	60%	10,915,045	29%	2,152,579	6%	1,485,030	4%	710,871	2%	38,280,810	4,970,489	9:02pm/10:02pm
May9/10:17pm	23,552,105	60%	11,133,118	29%	2,233,664	6%	1,512,344	4%	723,218	2%	39,204,447		
May9/10:32pm	24,070,851	60%	11,447,751	29%	2,316,665	6%	1,538,874	4%	733,999	2%	40,108,140		
May9/10:47pm	24,565,511	60%	11,691,138	29%	2,401,374	6%	1,563,170	4%	744,817	2%	40,966,010		
May9/11:02pm	25,051,855	60%	11,925,131	29%	2,484,310	6%	1,586,319	4%	754,869	2%	41,802,484	3,521,674	10:02pm/11:02pm
May9/11:17pm	25,489,420	60%	12,145,860	29%	2,564,260	6%	1,607,887	4%	763,927	2%	42,571,354		
May10/5:32am	30,223,129	60%	14,400,352	28%	3,451,398	7%	1,839,469	4%	864,197	2%	50,778,545	1,374,588	*
May13/3:18pm	31,104,175	59%	14,822,051	28%	3,629,805	7%	1,900,010	4%	882,236	2%	52,338,277	19,077	**

*From 11:02pm, May9 to 5:32am. May10 (Average per hour for 6.53 hours)

**From 5:32am, May10 to 3:18pm, May13 (Average per hour for 81.76 hours)

Pic1

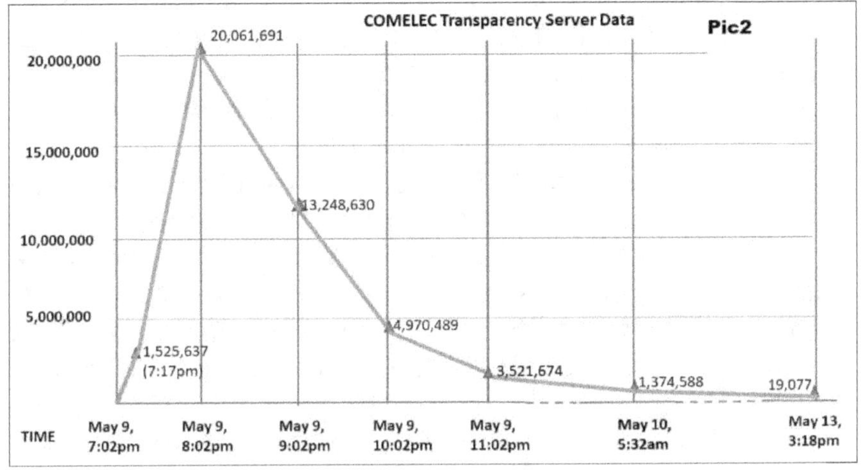

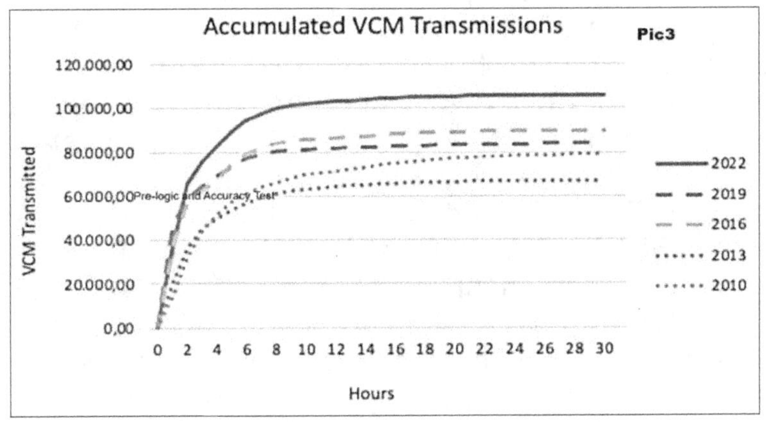

Eliseo Rio Jr

<u>56m</u> ·

"This is a much welcome development wherein all parties, including the COMELEC, will be able to conclusively respond to all issues under judicial processes," COMELEC Spokesperson John Rex Laudiangco said in a statement, referring to the mandamus petition we filed in the Supreme Court on November 3, 2022.

Laudiangco also reminded citizens who have issues concerning the electoral process that "the COMELEC Rules of Procedure, as well as the Rules on Civil Procedure (Rules of Court), provide for the proper avenues by which these may be properly ventilated within the ambit of due processes of law and public order."

Yet, we and the public wonder what due processes of law and public order will be affected by our simple request for COMELEC to show the public the time when VCM transmissions started on May 9, as shown below in their official "Accumulated VCM Transmissions" graph where the start is just designated as "0"?

It is our contention that the time indicated as "0", which in our assessment will not start earlier than 7:30pm because of the printing requirement of 8 copies of the precinct's Election Result (ER) before any VCM transmissions could be done, will prove beyond reasonable doubt our observation that the 20M+ votes shown to the public by the COMELEC Transparency Server at 8:02pm of May 9, just an hour after voting closed at 7pm, is extremely DUBIOUS IF NOT PRELOADED! If this unbelievable PEAK of 20M+ votes shown in the first hour of counting CAN NOT BE PROVEN BY ACTUAL VCM TRANSMISSIONS, then it would seem that the Transparency Server was used to condition the minds of the voting public what the "official" results of the election will be. IT WOULD MEAN THAT THE 2022 ELECTION MAY HAD BEEN RIGGED.

We have to go to the Supreme Court to petition that this time and other VCM transmission data be preserved, when COMELEC could have, weeks ago, easily shown the public in its website the time when VCM transmissions started on May 9, 2022 as shown in their own graph. IF THEY HAVE NOTHING TO HIDE, COMELEC WON'T BE INVOKING DUE PROCESS OF LAW AND PUBLIC ORDER TO VERY SIMPLE REQUESTS FROM CONCERNED CITIZENS.

oooooo

54
Update – Nov. 3, 2022 –
8PM – NYET –
Submission to SC

From our lawyer, we are sharing the official copy of our petition duly received by SC with time stamp dated November 3 and with assigned case number and filing fees for TRO

To lawyer intervenors, please take note the above case. There might be minimal filing fee for TRO.

Please advise us if you want to join our petition as intervenors so we can join forces.

Our truth warriors motto: " STRENGTH IN NUMBERS

6:47   .ıl LTE 🔋

Done **Petition for manda...**   🔍 Ⓐ

Republic of the Philippines
SUPREME COURT
Manila

SUPREME COURT
RECEIVED
BY :
2022 NOV -3 / AM 10: 34

En Banc

ELISEO MIJARES RIO JR. [1]
AUGUSTO CADELIÑA LAGMAN [2]
FRANKLIN FAYLOGA YSAAC [3]
      Petitioners

      versus   263838

COMMISSION ON ELECTIONS (COMELEC)
SMARTMATIC TOTAL INFORMATION MANAGEMENT
DITO TELECOMMUNITY
GLOBE TELECOM
SMART COMMUNICATIONS
      Respondents

PETITION
FOR MANDAMUS WITH PRAYER
FOR TEMPORARY RESTRAINING ORDER
TO COMPEL PRESERVATION AND/OR
RESTRAIN ALTERATION/ERASURE/DELETION OF
SUBSCRIBER AND CYBER TRAFFIC DATA INTEGRITY
OF TELECOM TRANSMISSIONS OF NATIONAL ELECTION RESULTS
FROM 7PM TO AT LEAST 9PM OF 09 MAY 2022 PHILIPPINES TIME

Petitioners, with the assistance of volunteer lawyers, most respectfully submit this politically-neutral urgent petition, involving transcendental national interest, unto the Honorable Supreme.

---

[1] DEPARTMENT OF INFORMATION & COMMUNICATIONS TECHNOLOGY (DICT) Secretary and COMELEC Advisory Council Chairman until 1 July 2019, NATIONAL TELECOMMUNICATIONS COMMISSION Commissioner (until 2003), Ret Brigadier General since 27 October 2000, Philippine Military Academy Instructor (until 1974), Electronics & Communications Engineer 1971 Board Exam 4th Placer

[2] COMELEC Commissioner (until 2012), NATIONAL MOVEMENT FOR FREE ELECTIONS (NAMFREL) President, Manila Times "Let's Face IT" Column Writer

[3] FINANCIAL EXECUTIVES INSTITUTE OF THE PHILIPPINES (FINEX) Former President, Software App Developer for Banks, Consultancies in the Bank of Saipan and select Banks in the Philippine, Franklin Financials Consultancy

---

PETITION TO COMPEL COMELEC SMARTMATIC TO PRESERVE SUBSCRIBER & CYBER TRAFFIC DATA INTEGRITY (RESTRAIN ERASURE) OF NATIONAL ELECTION RESULTS TRANSMITTED FROM 7PM TO AT LEAST 9PM OF 09 MAY 2022

Page 2 of 100

EXECUTIVE SUMMARY

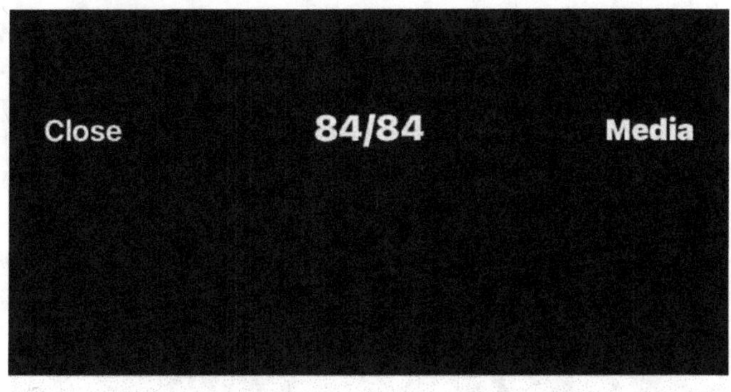

№ 347360 - SC - EP

(ORIGINAL)

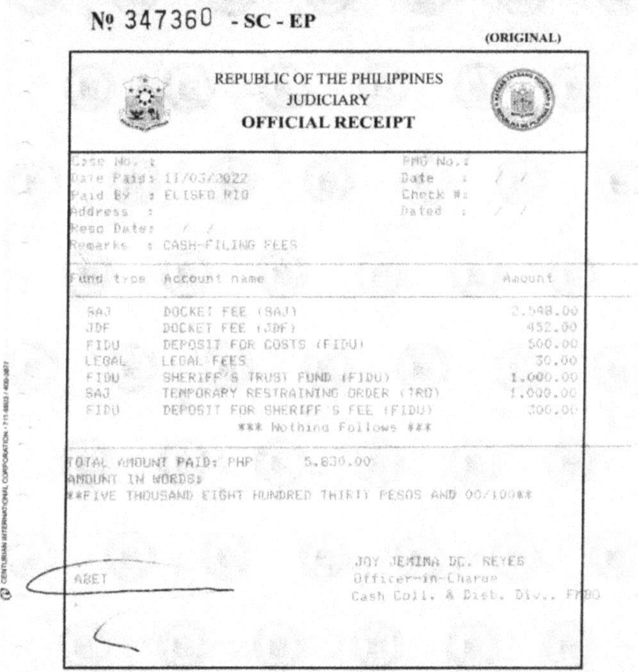

REPUBLIC OF THE PHILIPPINES
JUDICIARY
OFFICIAL RECEIPT

Case No. :
PMO No.:
Date Paid: 11/03/2022
Date : / /
Paid By : ELISEO RIO
Check #:
Address :
Dated : / /
Reso Date: / /
Remarks : CASH-FILING FEES

Fund type	Account name	Amount
SAJ	DOCKET FEE (SAJ)	2,548.00
JDF	DOCKET FEE (JDF)	452.00
FIDU	DEPOSIT FOR COSTS (FIDU)	500.00
LEGAL	LEGAL FEES	30.00
FIDU	SHERIFF'S TRUST FUND (FIDU)	1,000.00
SAJ	TEMPORARY RESTRAINING ORDER (TRO)	1,000.00
FIDU	DEPOSIT FOR SHERIFF'S FEE (FIDU)	300.00

*** Nothing Follows ***

TOTAL AMOUNT PAID: PHP 5,830.00
AMOUNT IN WORDS:
FIVE THOUSAND EIGHT HUNDRED THIRTY PESOS AND 00/100

JOY JEMIMA DC. REYES
Officer-in-Charge
Cash Coll. & Dist. Div., FMBO

6:47   LTE

Done **Petition for manda...**      

Republic of the Philippines
SUPREME COURT
Manila

En Banc

Eliseo Mijares Rio Jr. [1]
Augusto Cadeliña Lagman [2]
Franklin Fayloga Ysaac [3]
     Petitioners

     versus   263838

Commission on Elections (COMELEC)
Smartmatic Total Information Management
DITO Telecommunity
Globe Telecom
Smart Communications
     Respondents

PETITION

For Mandamus with Prayer
For Temporary Restraining Order
To Compel Preservation and/or
Restrain Alteration/Erasure/Deletion of
Subscriber and Cyber Traffic Data Integrity
of Telecom Transmissions of National Election Results
From 7PM to at least 9PM of 09 May 2022 Philippines Time

Petitioners, with the assistance of volunteer lawyers, most respectfully submit this politically-neutral urgent petition, involving transcendental national interest, unto the Honorable Supreme.

---

[1] Department of Information & Communications Technology (DICT) Secretary and COMELEC Advisory Council Chairman until 1 July 2019, National Telecommunications Commission Commissioner (until 2003), Ret Brigadier General since 27 October 2000, Philippine Military Academy Instructor (until 1974), Electronics & Communications Engineer 1971 Board Exam 4th Placer

[2] COMELEC Commissioner (until 2012), National Movement for Free Elections (NAMFREL) President, Manila Times "Let's Face IT" Column Writer

[3] Financial Executives Institute of the Philippines (FINEX) Former President, Software App Developer for Banks, Consultancies in the Bank of Saipan and select Banks in the Philippine, Franklin Financials Consultancy

EXECUTIVE SUMMARY

ooooooo

55
Update – Nov. 4, 2022 –
2PM – NYET –
TRO to safeguard Comelec records

Some of our truth warriors have been asking me what now after we filed the petition? What will happen next ? When is another rally ?

Let me just describe what we have accomplished yesterday . We followed the process of elevating our case to the SC after Comelec refused to grant our request last July 15, 2022. Second, the mainstream media has began to notice us and our truth campaign. They have been avoiding us like a plague before as they don't want their firms to be embroiled in the controversy like abs cbn. Third, the active response by truth warriors who came from the city and the nearby provinces just proved that our campaign is gaining nationwide recognition . Fourth, we have lawyer intervenors who promised to file similar case which is similar to our current case. Fifth, the event was carried in USA where millions of Filams reside and who have been following this campaign.

Post filing review of the mandamus and TRO case is the subject matter which will be taken up in the next meeting with our lawyers this coming week. A rundown or sequence of the election gave us a fighting chance as the first item that will be handled by SC is the TRO.

According to our lawyer who worked before with the SC, on the day of filing, the SC will decide who amongst the justices will be the ponente who will handle the case . Once this is determined on day 1, the next step is the justice assigned will recommend whether the first item in the petition which is TRO may be issued with one signature or with two other justices in his / her division . The TRO will have a deadline on its own. In this case,we will request for at least six more months.

We will be taking up the case of ppcrv in this meeting and we will assist our warrior lawyers who will act as intervenors.

Per our lawyer, this is a different and an unprecedented case and is not subject to sub judice rule. Let's just avoid using those words in our posts that will invite unnecessary or untoward incidents.

We will discuss other important matters in the next update.

oooooo

56
Update – Nov. 4, 2022 -
Comelec Lawyer on IT matters

A lawyer with no or barely enough knowledge about IT cannot be spokesman for IT matters . In the same manner, an IT cannot be spokesman for legal matters.

That's why we IT experts work hand in hand with legal experts to ensure we are on safe ground, from IT to Legal Ground.

Since Comelec refused to answer our July 15 letter directly, now they find themselves in a quandary or in a hole where they exposed themselves about irregularities they cannot defend.

Let's see how they will respond to our petition which is now in the hands of the SC.

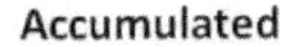
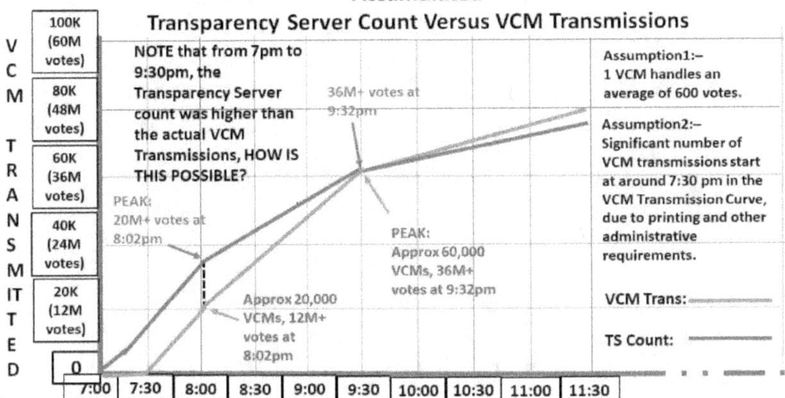

Date/Time	BBM votes	BBM%	Leni votes	Leni%	Paq votes	Paq%	Isko votes	Isko%	Ping votes	Ping%	Total	Hourly +Votes	From/To
May 9/7:02pm	0	0%	0	0%	0	0%	0	0%	0	0%	0	0	
May 9/7:17pm	958,219	63%	409,608	27%	76,668	5%	54,755	4%	26,387	2%	1,525,637		
May 9/8:01pm	12,065,875	60%	5,756,125	29%	957,851	5%	874,188	4%	407,652	2%	20,061,691	20,061,691	7:02pm/8:02pm
May9/8:17pm	15,339,876	60%	7,288,834	29%	1,262,192	5%	1,063,656	4%	505,265	2%	21,459,825		
May9/8:32pm	17,541,799	60%	8,311,501	29%	1,486,592	5%	1,188,776	4%	567,761	2%	29,096,429		
May9/8:47pm	18,975,119	60%	8,979,607	29%	1,639,533	5%	1,268,386	4%	607,251	2%	31,469,898		
May9/9:02pm	20,064,651	60%	9,492,702	28%	1,766,290	5%	1,330,088	4%	636,590	2%	33,210,321	13,248,630	8:02pm/9:02pm
May9/9:17pm	20,978,083	60%	9,921,820	28%	1,879,407	5%	1,378,744	4%	660,178	2%	34,818,232		
May9/9:32pm	21,725,982	60%	10,282,280	28%	1,974,234	5%	1,418,809	4%	679,229	2%	36,080,534		
May9/9:47pm	22,410,199	60%	10,613,144	28%	2,066,021	6%	1,453,828	4%	696,040	2%	37,239,232		
May9/10:02pm	28,017,285	60%	10,915,045	29%	2,132,579	6%	1,485,030	4%	710,871	2%	38,280,810	4,970,489	9:02pm/10:02pm
May9/10:17pm	29,552,103	60%	11,183,118	29%	2,233,664	6%	1,512,344	4%	721,218	2%	39,204,447		
May9/10:32pm	24,070,851	60%	11,447,751	29%	2,316,665	6%	1,538,874	4%	733,999	2%	40,108,140		
May9/10:47pm	24,565,311	60%	11,691,138	29%	2,401,374	6%	1,563,170	4%	744,817	2%	40,966,010		
May9/11:02pm	25,051,855	60%	11,915,181	29%	2,484,310	6%	1,586,819	4%	754,869	2%	41,802,484	3,521,674	10:02pm/11:02pm
May9/11:17pm	25,489,420	60%	12,145,860	29%	2,564,260	6%	1,607,887	4%	763,927	2%	42,571,354		
May10/5:32am	30,223,129	60%	14,400,352	28%	3,451,393	7%	1,833,469	4%	864,197	2%	50,778,545	1,374,588	*
May13/3:18pm	31,104,175	59%	14,822,051	28%	3,629,805	7%	1,900,010	4%	882,236	2%	52,338,277	19,077	**

*From 11:02pm, May9 to 5:32am, May10 (Average per hour for 6.53 hours)

**From 5:52am, May10 to 3:18pm, May13 (Average per hour for 81.76 hours)

Pic1

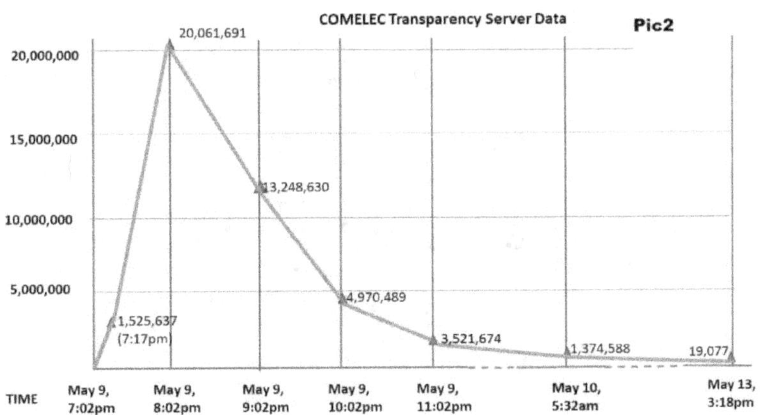

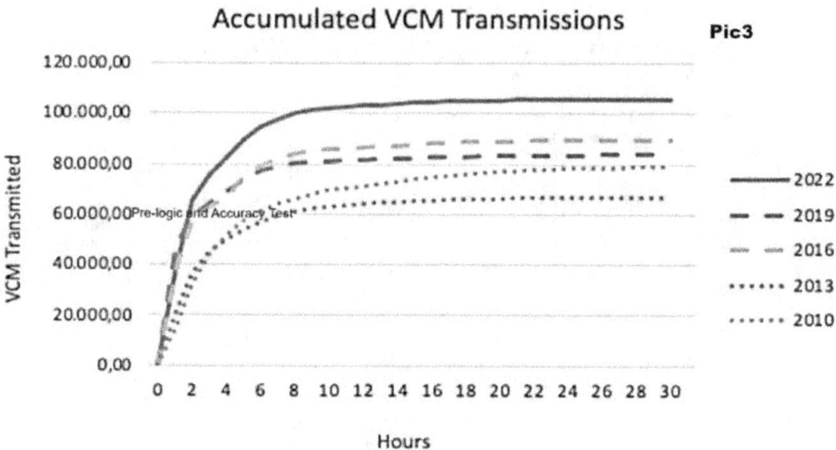

(Rio vs Comelec lawyer exchange – temporarily lost space)

oooooo

57
Update – Nov. 4, 2022 –
6PM – NYET
Next Moves

Many of our truth warriors continue to follow up with us re our next moves.

I already described the SC process. We are expressing our trust that SC will grant the TRO on the telcos to preserve the transmission data, if any, from vcm to transparency and central servers during the first hour early next week before November 9 deadline as we have already complied with requirements for issuance of TRO and we have paid TRO fees. The issuance can either be issued by the assigned SC ponente alone or with two justices in their division.

What is critical is the mandamus which has to be decided en banc under SC rules. But prior to that, the SC will request the respondents to comment on our petition. Our petition is comprehensive enough to answer any of contrary allegations by the respondents. This may take some time as the normal period for response is 10 days. Then we have to make our response to their response. These will be all via letters or memorandum. Every SC justice and respondents will have copies of these exchanges. Physical hearing may be required depending on what the SC justices desire if they want clarifications from us. Otherwise, these exchanges should not go beyond one month or maximum two months as this is not an ordinary petition but a petition of the Filipino people which has impact on the credibility of election which all voters are entitled to know under the freedom of information act. We mentioned this already in our petition as our basis for our request for transmission data from Comelec.

We shall be updating all of any development coming from the SC.

Let's continue praying for the Almighty to guide and ensure there won't be any delay on this people's petiton for truth and transparency.

Amen.

oooooo

58
Update – Nov. 4, 2022 –
7PM – NYET- Lincoln

This is the great American President who speaks with grains of truth and his words echo throughout American history.

We echo the same words in our truth campaign.

May kasabihan Sabi ng Papa ko na isang sundalo " lahat ng bagay May katapat ". Ang isang masamang tao ay may makakatapat sa kanyang panahon. Kaya anak, mag pakabuti kang tao. Wag kang magnakaw . Wag kang manakit ng tao . Mahalin mo ang sarili mo at pamilya mo at kaibigan kahit mga kaaway o katunggali mo. " I was only in my teen and I was about to graduate HS when the good Lord took him away from us."

To Papa, Eto po anak niyo nagsisilbi sa bayan. Hindi po ako magnakaw Kailan man. Hindi po ako nanakit ng tao. Pero pinaglalaban ko Papa ang katotohanan, ang karapatan ng taong inaapi at Yung gustong agawin ang pinaghirapan ko lumalaban ako sa korte. Hindi man ako naging abogado Pero nag aral ako ng mga batas lalo na banking laws . At sa mga kasong sinampa ko siniguro ko mananalo ako. At tagumpay ako kasi inaaral ko kaso ko.

Kaya etong petition natin sa korte suprema Natuto pa ako sa magagaling nating mga abogado

Ang nagmamahal na Yung bunsong lalaki mong anak,

Panky or Patty as I was known to my family and friends !

This is the great American President who speaks with grains of truth and his words echo throughout American history.

We echo the same words in our truth campaign.

My Papa said a soldier " everything has a limit ". A bad person will have his time wasted. That's why, my child, be a good person. Do not steal. Don't hurt people. Love yourself and your family and friends even your enemies or foes. I was only in my teens and I was about to graduate HS when the good Lord took him …

GOODREADS.COM

A quote by Abraham Lincoln
You can fool some of the people all of the time, and all of the people some of the time, but you can not fool all of the people all of the time.

oooooo

59
Update – Nov. 5, 2022 –
7AM-NYET –
If Supreme Court Denies Petition?

Hindi ko po maiwasan ang mga katanungan at Marami sa mga nag susubaybay sa post namin kung sakali ma bigyan ng daan ng SC ang kahilingan natin at Wala talaga mabigay ang Comelec ng hinihingi natin, nag speculate na po sila .

Kung mapatunayan na May dayaan noong eleksyon sa pamamagitan ng pag areglo ng transparency server, Sabi nila Dapat daw manalo ang Hindi nandaya.

Ganito po yan . Ang Sabi ng mga abogado na kapag mapatunayan na May malaking dayaan Hindi Basta uupo ang Pangalawa. Ang susunod na Kilos po daw ay mag file another petition to possibly request for another election but this is contentious po.

Marami pa po Pwede mangyari.

Papano pag deny ang petition natin. Yan po ang Pinagusapan namin

Kaya po sa court of public opinion at ang taumbayan na po mag husga .

(Translation)

I can't avoid the questions and many of those who are following our post just in case the SC will grant our request and Comelec can't really give us what we are asking for, they are already speculating.

If it can be proven that there was cheating during the election by fixing the transparency server, they said that the one who didn't cheat should win.

This is how it is. Lawyers say that if it is proven that there is big fraud, the second will not just sit. The next move is to file another petition to possibly request for another election but this is contentious.

More can happen.

What if our petition is denied? That's what we talked about

That's why the court of public opinion and the people will judge.

oooooo

60
Update – Nov. 5, 2022 –
8PM – NYET –
The Public Deserve to know the truth

To all,

Please be advised that after our much publicized filing of a simple case of requesting the SC of issuing a TRO on telcos preserving transmission logs and the Comelec delivering the transmission data, there are some quarters making the rounds debunking our petition that it is baseless and untrue.

Our position is very clear. We have been engaging debates on the possibility of fraud during the last election and the Ateneo debate last month gave away the position of Comelec where the graph the comelec chair showed proved there were no 21 million votes counted in favor of the incumbent.

That revelation is included in our petition where we requested the SC to mandate Comelec to submit transmission data and reports to prove their point.

Some camps including trolls are trying to discredit our position and we will not fall into a trap to answer back. Even alleged iT experts and academe from certain schools are challenging our position. If these people want a debate, they can appear in court as lawyer for the other camp.

We like to emphasize that since the case is now in court, let's refrain from making any further comments which both camps may use against each other.

As we have said from the very beginning, this is not a political protest where a candidate is challenging the results of the election. It's a very simple case where the comelec and the telcos are being requested to follow our petition for TRO and submission of transmission reports which we, ordinary voters, are entitled to know because that is our inherent right to know under freedom of information law. This is well defended in our premise in our petition.

Turning against this position or denying us our petition means the officials responsible for election conduct with transparency is hiding the truth from the millions of voters. Already, we requested this from them since July 15, 2022 and they ignored our request and they told us to go to Comelec advisory council and Joint Congressional Oversight Cmte on Automated Election which we followed and until now there was no response.

If Comelec only truthfully answered our request and also requests from truth warriors, then we would not have filed this request before the SC.

It's up to the SC to give and respect the Filipino people's right to know the truth.

Denying the truth means they are hiding the truth from us.

The Filipino people, through our efforts, have already spoken and we #TNTrio have given a chance to Comelec to answer our request directly and categorically and they lost that chance.

We request the Filipino people to become vigilant and to pray before the SC to make decision before November 9 date starting Monday November 7 through Wednesday November 9.

Beyond that date, we need more voices from the Filipino people to pray that the mandamus petition will be granted by the SC.

We want more from our truth warrior lawyers to come forward to submit the same position before the SC as lawyer intervenors for our cause.

The pressure is on and we #TNTrio are appealing to all to be one and united in this unprecedented case.

We are looking at the mandamus to be the litmus test of our case and we are constrained to keep our brave lawyers and we need to sustain our support for them financially as they have set aside their other important cases as they realize this case is a case that cannot be set aside as this is a transcendental case that affects every Filipino who wants the truth to come out.

Let the truth begin and we implore and invoke the Holy Spirit to continue to guide our brave lawyers and the SC to be enlightened and prove to the Filipino people that truth matters and the Filipino people's rights matter.

Amen.

oooooo